C000261793

Jesus the Deliverer

John Linden-Cook

New Wine Press

New Wine Press
PO Box 17
Chichester
West Sussex
PO20 6YB
England

All Scripture quotations are taken from the New King James
Version, copyright © 1983 by Thomas Nelson, Inc.

ISBN: 1 874367 38 8

Typeset by CRB Associates, Lenwade, Norwich
Printed in England by Clays Ltd, St Ives plc

Contents

Acknowledgements

Firstly, I would like to thank Tony Derrick, a professional journalist of over 25 years standing, for his painstaking work in editing the material for this book, without which it would never have appeared in print; also for his many helpful suggestions and advice. He has spent many hours listening to cassettes of our teaching material and has checked every page in line with what he has heard.

Secondly, my thanks are due to my wife, Elsa, who has also had much input to the manuscript of this book. In particular Chapter 3 is her work as is also the story of 'Ginger' which appears towards the end.

Above all I thank the Lord Jesus for laying it on our hearts to write this book which we trust will be a useful teaching resource. It is our prayer that you, who read this book, will be encouraged in your faith and be able to trust fully in the Lord Jesus and in His written and inspired word, the Bible.

Jesus said:

> *'Heaven and earth will pass away, but My words will never pass away.'*

John Linden-Cook

Foreword

What we are up against

It is a commonly held view that Christianity consists of going to church regularly, singing hymns, saying formal prayers, doing something to help other people and raising money by means of jumble sales and bazaars to pay for the repair of the church steeple or the organ.

These things certainly feature in church life, but they hide from us the basic struggle we are in. We are all involved, either consciously and willingly, or unwillingly and without realising it, in spiritual warfare. There is a continuing warfare between good and evil in men's hearts and in the circumstances of our lives. As soon as we give our allegiance to Jesus by committing ourselves as Christians, we have taken up opposition to the enemy and can expect him to react. While we are, as we imagine, neutral, he has nothing to fear from us. In fact, we are putty in his hands. But from the moment we oppose him, he swings into action against us to trip us up, block our progress, discourage us, tire us out by overworking us, deceive us, and destroy us if he can.

Any concept of the Christian life that does not take full account of this warfare is faulty and out of touch with reality. We **are** in a war, so we have to inform ourselves about our enemy's tactics and the spiritual resources and techniques our Saviour has equipped us with – not merely to defend ourselves, but to defeat the enemy. For here is a further misconception that is widespread – that the church is on the defensive. Jesus said quite plainly that *'the gates of hell shall not prevail against it'*, which surely makes it plain that He intended us to be on the offensive. (Note that the gates of a city in biblical times were the meeting place of the city council, the ruling authorities.)

We must, then, wake from our sleep. We must not be so easily satisfied with just 'getting by' in the Christian life or with making modest gains for the Kingdom. Jesus intends us to be **overcomers**. Yet at the same time we must not expect this to be easy. We need to submit ourselves to God's timing in these matters and be prepared if necessary for great effort and endurance and sacrifice over an extended period before victory is achieved – though sometimes, praise the Lord, victory may come quickly and unexpectedly.

Wait upon God. Keep close to Him and He will reveal His plans and His methods to you, so far as you need to know them. Some advances against the enemy will be made quickly and surprisingly easily because they are done with the means and the powers the Lord provides – notably words of knowledge and the use of the powerful Name and authority of Jesus. Others will require lengthy persistence and sometimes even years of spiritual growth and maturing in ourselves before victory can be gained. But throughout we must appreciate we are warriors and potential victors. That is what the Lord intends for us.

This book is basically a teaching book, setting out the lessons John and Elsa Linden-Cook have learned from over 30 years of experience and, yes, battle. But it is important that you, the readers, take on board what is said, in the most effective way. There is much knowledge, based on the Bible and on these experiences, themselves checked out with the Bible, which you need to know. But you should not just fill out your knowledge and stay sitting in your chair or pew. You should take these things on board as additional weapons or ammunition to use in the spiritual war in which you are engaged.

Never think of Satan as a gentlemanly opponent whom you spar with, as in some kind of sport. The Bible tells us – so we had better take note of it! – that he prowls round looking for someone to devour. His aim is to steal, kill and destroy. So expect a 'no-holds-barred' enemy, a dirty fighter, and mobilise all your spiritual resources to counter him. Remember, as in total warfare on earth, it is **him** or **you**. Make sure it is not you!

Tony Derrick

Chapter 1

How it all Began

Churchianity – my spiritual sickness

'You won't get another chance.' In the silence of that small church near Trafalgar Square in London the voice was clear and firm. Deep down in my heart I knew who was speaking, although I had never heard His voice before. He had no doubt spoken to me, but I had not been listening. It is strange – you can go to church for years, pray, say and do all the so-called right things, yet never know the One whose house it is. Unbeknown to me, God's plan for my life was about to unfold. It is as well I did not know then what paths it would lead me into. I had felt uncomfortable in that small church when we came the previous evening. Not surprising, as I had been brought up in the true Anglican tradition in a not particularly evangelical church. Attending church each Sunday was part of life's routine and held little meaning for me. It was just one of those things one did. At home the Bible was not read, except by my mother when she was alone. Prayer was reserved for those few moments before climbing into bed – all rather perfunctory, with little real meaning or purpose. I had just been taught to do it and was required to by my mother.

I was involved in most of the church's activities – Boy Scouts, Youth Fellowship, a member of the choir (from a very early age) and so on. But somehow the deeper meaning and purpose of it all escaped me. I had been baptised and confirmed, because that was what young people were supposed to do. Within my limits, I tried to live a reasonably good life, not always very successfully. As I viewed it, all that was necessary was to live a 'good' life, be a kind neighbour when required, attend church fairly regularly – after all we should show some respect for God – and generally try to be a good citizen. Even becoming a church organist and choirmaster was just another church activity for me. Being on the electoral roll of my Parish entitled me, of course, to go to heaven when this life was over!

I continued to go to church during my apprenticeship as a printing compositor and at $17\frac{1}{2}$ years of age I volunteered for the Royal Navy and was accepted for training as a Telegraphist. During this time I went to church fairly regularly. I had formed a friendship with another young man from Harrogate, who was a bellringer, so we went together. He hoped to be able to ring the bells, I hoped to be allowed to play the organ at some point – something I still enjoy whenever an opportunity presents itself.

After my training I was sent to Freetown, West Africa, to the main signal station. During this time I caught dysentery and some months later I went down with malignant malaria. This was nearly the end of me. The Padre was informed of my condition so that he could send the usual letter to my parents telling them I had passed away, but God had other plans. After some 36 hours, during which my life hung in the balance, I awoke, much to the surprise of the orderly who was sitting by my bed waiting for the end. After about six months it was back home.

12

But the malaria caused me many bouts of fever and ache. Though it appeared to have gone, it troubled me on and off for many years. But then the Lord delivered me, and it has never returned.

Some years later I started work in London and it was here I met my future wife, Elsa, who was a visitor from Germany. We went out together and a few years later we were married. Our smoking habit was a great drain on our finances – but we liked it that way. I had now moved on to work in an advertising agency as Print Buyer and not long after that I became Sales Director for a small printing group.

1962 – Is the Bible true or false?

Home life with Elsa was very good and although neither of us was particularly religious, we went to church quite often. I think Elsa already knew Jesus then, but certainly I didn't. Because of our circumstances it was not possible for us to go to Germany together each year on holiday, so Elsa went alone. One year she came back with a modern translation of the Bible. Sitting at home in the evenings, she often read it while I read the paper or a magazine. From time to time she would ask me to listen while she read something from her new Bible. Now I was brought up on the 1662 Bible and the 1928 Prayer Book, neither of which meant a great deal to Elsa, as she came from Germany, so when translating for me she put it into modern English. I began to get interested because, for the first time in my life, the Bible was beginning to make sense. I became intrigued and we finally went out and bought me a modern version of the New Testament by J.B. Phillips.

As I read I found that the life of Jesus was marked time and time again by miracles. He cast out demons,

He healed the sick, stilled storms and raised the dead. The Bible taught that He was still alive today and so, I reasoned, He ought to be doing the same things today. The Bible clearly stated that He *'is the same yesterday, today, and forever'* (Hebrews 13:8). If this statement was true, where were all these miracles taking place in our day? Certainly not in any of the churches I had been to. Our quest began. We visited many churches of various denominations and, as the custom was, the minister usually walked to the back of the church after the service to bid people goodbye. When it came to our turn he usually asked politely if we had enjoyed the meeting, or were visiting the area or recently moved there.

I had a question. In reading the Bible I had found in Matthew that Jesus healed the sick and cast out demons and so on. Mark and Luke recorded the same sort of things. I had read on into John and found a similar narrative until I reached John 14:12. There I read,

> *'Most assuredly, I say to you, he who believes in Me, the works that I do he will do also; and greater works than these he will do, because I go to My Father.'*

For a long time I had pondered this. Was it true – **really** true? Did Jesus really mean what He was saying? Was it possible that those who believed in Him would do the same things He was doing and had done? I turned back to the end of Mark's Gospel and read again what he had written:

> *'These signs will follow those who believe; In My name they will cast out demons ... they will lay hands on the sick and they will recover.'*

Finally I read on from John's Gospel and in 1 Corinthians 12 discovered there was a gift of healing and also a gift of miracles. In the Book of Acts the disciples had done similar works to those done by Jesus Himself – even to raising the dead!

My question to the ministers of the various churches we visited was always the same: 'When do you pray for the sick and cast out demons in your church?' Always the reply was the same: 'What do you mean, "When do we pray for the sick and cast out demons"?' I would then quote the verse in John's Gospel and infer that as Jesus had done that sort of thing, when did they do it? The answer usually took the form, 'Ah, well, you see Brother, we don't need healing miracles today. We have the doctors and the psychiatrists and the psychologists, the hospitals and the nurses. No, we don't need miracles today!' I was perplexed. Was John 14:12 true or false? Could we rely on the accuracy of the Bible or should we dismiss some of it as irrelevant or inaccurate or just not for today? If we could not rely on its accuracy, if it was irrelevant, and parts of it were just not for today, how should we know **which** parts were irrelevant, inaccurate or not for today? What do you take out and what do you leave in – and how do you decide? I wanted an answer to my question, 'Is John 14:12 true or false?' but it seemed as if no one knew the answer. My church upbringing had taught me that the Bible was true, yet here were ministers of various denominations avoiding a direct answer. Miracles of healing and casting out demons, it seemed, were not for today – or were they? I had almost reached the point of deciding that the Bible was not totally true after all, when God stepped in.

A business meeting arranged by God

One day, after concluding my business as a printing Sales Director with a client, I was getting up to go when she said, 'Sit down. I want to ask you a question.' I sat down. 'Are you saved?' she asked. 'Do you know Jesus as your personal Saviour?' Somewhat taken aback, I played for time. 'What do you mean?' I countered. 'Do you know Jesus in a personal way? Have you met Him? Have you had a personal encounter with the risen Christ?' By now I had got my breath back and, drawing myself up to my full height (sitting in a chair!), I said, 'I am an Anglican, on the electoral roll of my Parish.' For good measure I added that I had also been confirmed. 'Oh, I don't mean that,' she said. 'Have you had your sins forgiven?' I was out of my depth but had a sudden brainwave. I know, I'll ask her my question. So I said, 'It seems to me that the Bible is not all true, because it says that Jesus healed all who were sick. It also says that He is always the same. Yet where are the healings today? What am I to think? It is very difficult to believe in a God who says something and then changes His mind!' We discussed my question to the various church ministers, then she quietly took a leaflet from her desk drawer and said to me, 'If you would like to go to those meetings, you will see blind eyes opened and the lame walking.' That had been my challenge – I wanted to see blind eyes opened and the lame walking. We need to be careful how we challenge God for He will often take us up on it. He took me up on mine! The meetings were due to start the following Monday evening. We went.

Signs follow preaching of the Word

The evangelist no doubt gave a good message, but I failed to hear any of it – I had not gone to listen but to see. It had been an odd meeting for me. There was a very nice pipe organ at the front of the church, yet they chose to use a honky tonk piano. This did not go down too well with the organist in me! They did not sing anything I had heard before – nothing from *Hymns Ancient and Modern*. Prayer was offered by any who felt so led, whereas in my church only the Vicar prayed and we all said 'Amen'. Some had tambourines and the people seemed to be happy – and that in church! I was certainly not used to this. At one point I felt as if we should go home. It seemed no place for Elsa and me. But having come, we stayed. When the speaker asked those who needed healing to come forward, I paid close attention. This was what I had come for and I was determined not to miss any of it. The blind eyes opened, indeed!

The first one to be prayed for was a lady who was blind in one eye. The evangelist prayed for her and then, blocking out her good eye with his hand, turned her round to face us all and asked her, 'What is the time by that clock at the back of the church?' 'It's nearly half past ... I can see!' she cried out. Now it was my custom in any strange church always to sit on the end of a pew and this was no exception. The lady was so overjoyed at what had happened to her that, leaving gloves and hand-bag at the front of the church, she came down the aisle and wherever someone was sitting on the end of a pew, she put her face close to theirs and said, 'I can see!' She did the same to me. It was obvious that she could see out of both eyes! The next one was lame. After prayer he ran down the aisle apparently healed, which he claimed to be. I had no reason to doubt it. We saw many other miracles that night and went home in a sober mood with much to think about.

Touched by Jesus

We decided to go back on the Tuesday evening, 3rd December, 1962. He preached on the text of the woman who had an issue of blood for 12 years and was healed when she touched the hem of Jesus' garment (Matthew 9:20–22). At the end of his message he said, 'We are going to call the sick forward in a moment, but before we do, there are those here tonight who have a greater need. They need to know Jesus as their Saviour and Lord. They need to be forgiven for their sins.' He asked everyone to close their eyes and not look around. Then he asked those who wanted to know Jesus personally to raise their right hands. He would acknowledge this, then they could put them down again. This is not for me, I thought. I'm all right. But then the doubts started. The Holy Spirit was at work and slowly revealed to me that I was indeed a sinner in need of a Saviour. I was not born again, despite my churchianity.

For the first time in my life I began to see myself as God saw me. My self-righteousness began to crumble and I realised that I was not, after all, bound for heaven, but for hell! The evangelist was still speaking. No one had, as yet, responded to his invitation. It was then, in a few moments of silence while the evangelist waited for the first response to his call, that I heard those words, 'You won't get another chance.' I decided I must put my hand up. But wait! – Elsa was sitting beside me and the man had said that this was to be just between him and us and the Lord, with no one looking around. In a flash of insight I suddenly realised that if I raised my hand my clothes would rustle. Grateful that we were sitting on benches, I was able to slide a little away from Elsa and very slowly and gingerly raised my arm. 'I see you brother!' It seemed as if he had shouted the words in that silent church. My arm shot down. I felt awful – hot and cold all over. A few more raised their hands and he acknowledged them quite quietly it seemed.

18

After this, he asked those who had put their hands up to come forward. 'Oh no,' I thought. Then, to my surprise, Elsa stood up. I had not heard her put her hand up. Together we went to the front. He spoke to Elsa first and she said a very simple prayer, inviting the Lord Jesus into her heart and life, and was truly born again. Then he stood in front of me. As I asked God to forgive my sinful past it was as if a hundredweight burden fell off my back. Inside I felt clean. It was an amazing experience and I knew that I, too, was truly born again. Then he did something he did not normally do. We attended many of the meetings and so realised later that what he did next was unusual. 'Is there something else you want from the Lord?' 'Yes, there is,' I replied. 'I have a lung complaint, and it is killing me.' He said, 'I will pray for you now' and proceeded to do so. It was as if 600 volts of electricity went through me everywhere. The sickness has gone and never returned, for which we praise the Lord Jesus.

Lifted into the presence of Jesus

Some months after this experience I was back in the same church, this time wanting to receive the fullness of the Holy Spirit. We had been to so many meetings by now and seen the power of God in action. Oh yes, the Bible was true all right – and I wanted to be part of it. That night was to be another turning point. I little knew just what God had in store for me but I knew I needed that infilling of the Holy Spirit which my wife had received some months earlier. So many had prayed for me to receive the gift of the Holy Spirit, yet nothing ever happened. I always went home the same as I arrived. One day in desperation I cried out to God on my knees in a City of London church and He answered me. 'Why can't I receive it, Lord? What's in the way?' 'You,' came back the reply in that same clear, firm voice I had heard in the church that night I was born again. The Lord Jesus and I spent some three months going through my life. He showed me many things which I still needed to repent of and many people I needed to forgive. But at last I felt really ready and said to Elsa, 'We will go on Saturday evening. I am sure I will receive the Holy Spirit then.' We went and saw many healings and people coming forward for salvation.

Then it came: 'If there is anyone here tonight,' the evangelist said, 'Who wants to receive the fullness of the Holy Spirit, just come and sit in the front here and we will come and pray for you.' I was there! Nobody else came. The evangelist looked at me, rather pityingly I felt, and said, 'Brother, we have prayed with you so many times, I am not coming down there to pray with you tonight. Just receive the Holy Spirit.' I was furious. He had prayed with me many times, so surely once more would not hurt. By now he had walked to the back of the church and so I got up and went to remonstrate with him. He just told me to go and sit down and talk to the Lord about it. I did. Firstly I knew I had to repent of the anger against the evangelist, so I did just that. Then came that Voice again. 'Well?' He said. 'Yes, Lord. Please take me.' He did. I had my eyes closed all this time and felt as though I was lifted into His very presence. I began worshipping Him in a heavenly tongue – this ended with what Elsa afterwards called a laughter of pure joy which blessed the few people who were still in the church. All the others had gone home and the caretaker was waiting to lock up. David Foot was the man who had arranged these meetings and I am eternally grateful to him for being obedient to the calling God gave him to do this. Had it not been for these meetings I wonder whether I

20

would have ever been born again? Only the Lord Jesus knows the answer to that question.

His Word confirmed

I had truly been baptised in the Holy Spirit and I felt His love in me and I was very eager to pray for the sick and see the hospitals emptied! It was only later I realised that God does not work in that way! However, it was not long after this wonderful experience that I had the great blessing of praying for a young boy of about 14 who was suffering from gangrene in his leg. It was getting worse and the hospital doctors had said that the only answer to stopping it from spreading elsewhere, was to amputate his leg just below the knee. He loved playing football for one thing and there would have been a permanent disablement from such an operation. After prayer he went home and a few days later went to the hospital again for what was to have been his last examination before the operation. The weeping in the wound had started easing up and as there were obvious signs of healing the doctors decided to leave it for the present and put new dressings on and see how things went. A few weeks later you could hardly see where the wound had been. It proved to be the beginning of a ministry which has spanned over 30 years.

I had been allowed to taste of heavenly powers and I greatly rejoiced. It was not long after this that I began to understand what the Apostle Paul meant when he wrote to the Ephesians:

> *'For we do not wrestle against flesh and blood, but against principalities, against powers, against the rulers of the darkness of this age, against spiritual hosts of wickedness in the heavenly places.'*

21

There exists a spiritual world, much greater than this world of ours – but also there is a war being waged between the heavenly hosts and the satanic angels. And we have been given power and authority to join in this fight with a certainty of victory through our Lord Jesus Christ.

Chapter 2

Good News!

The prime purpose of our ministry is to lead people out of spiritual darkness into the light and set them free, spiritually, mentally, emotionally and physically, so they can fulfil God's purposes for their lives without hindrance. For a ministry to be truly effective and reliable, it must be firmly based on God's laws, words and promises, as recorded in Scripture.

We are most careful to minister and teach in this way, so that we walk a sure path. We can then say to anyone who questions or opposes our teaching, 'Don't take our word for it. Consider what God says in His word and accept that – or reject it at your peril.' So we cannot do better than take a close look at Jesus' ministry.

Jesus was anointed to preach good news, good tidings to the poor. In the Nazareth synagogue He read from Isaiah 61:1–2a:

> *'The Spirit of the Lord God is upon Me, because the Lord has anointed Me to preach good tidings to the poor; He has sent Me to heal the brokenhearted, to proclaim liberty to the captives, and the opening of the prison to those who are bound; to proclaim the acceptable year of the Lord.'*

But what are the good tidings? We find the answer in Acts 26:13, 18, where Paul is struck down on the road to Damascus. *'Saul, Saul, why are you persecuting Me?'* Jesus asks. Then in verse 18 He explains,

> *'I now send you* (to the Jews and the Gentiles), *to open their eyes and to turn them from darkness to light, and from the power of Satan to God, that they may receive forgiveness of sins and an inheritance among those who are sanctified by faith in Me.'*

Our faith has to be in Jesus. We never get sanctified by faith in someone else, least of all ourselves.

Jesus came and preached Himself and the Kingdom of God, and He is the only way into that Kingdom. He said,

> *'I am the way, the truth, and the life. No one comes to the Father except through Me.'*   (John 14:6)

These days we have the New Age movement, 'the god within', 'reach your potential', 'you will be like God', like Genesis 3:5. According to New Age teaching we are gods in the making. We only have to release our potential. Do you realise that? Well, that is a lie. The only way to release your potential is to be in Jesus, to be sanctified by faith in Jesus. There is only one path to God, and that is in Jesus.

Jesus alone is the Way and that is **good news**, because we have a sure and certain way to God. Jesus is in heaven where He sits at the right hand of the Father. We do not have to deal with a dead body because God raised Jesus from the dead. This is the good news. For the Christian there is good news even when we come to

24

death, because there is resurrection for us. If we believe in Jesus and are alive when He comes for us, we shall never die. I'm not looking for a coffin, because I expect Jesus to come back in my lifetime – probably in less than ten years. If I'm right, that is good news. But it is still good news if I am wrong, because He is certainly coming one day and when He does I shall be resurrected along with all those who are born again and belong to Him.

We need to get this good news to people out there. So many people are afraid. Why do you think people sit glued to the television? Why do they go into pornography? Why do they go into satanic things? Why do they go into the New Age movement? Why do they become Buddhists, Rosicrucians, Freemasons, or whatever? It is because Satan has blinded their eyes. They are in darkness and they don't want to think about God. 'Give me anything, but don't let me think about God. Just keep me occupied. Let me dance, let me sing, let me watch a movie ... but don't let me stop and have to think about God.' The good news is that if they **would** only stop and think about God, He would release them from all that rubbish. They would be set free of it.

Before we can minister, **we need to know the basis of our good news**. We need to know who we are in Christ Jesus – sons and heirs of God, empowered and protected from evil – and what our anointing is in Him. Paul tells the Corinthians that both they and he are established in Christ and anointed by God (2 Corinthians 1:21) and John in his first letter (1 John 2:27) tells his readers that they have received an anointing from the Lord Jesus. We have been chosen by the Lord Jesus Himself that we should go and bear much fruit. The anointing is that of the Holy Spirit and in the Book of Acts Peter, in the house of Cornelius, says,

'God anointed Jesus of Nazareth with the Holy Spirit and with power, who went about doing good and healing all who were oppressed by the devil, for God was with Him.'

And the Holy Spirit is with us and upon us anointing us for the same works that Jesus Himself did – was this not His promise in John 14:12 which led to my own conversion? This is the basis of our good news.

Jesus came to bring good news to the poor – and before we are born again we are very poor, however much money we have. We are absolute paupers. All of us are in the kingdom of Satan before we are born again. Everyone is until he or she is born again. Before I was born again I was a child of the devil.

You *must* be born again

The Bible says the whole world lies in the grip of the evil one. You, dear reader, were once in his grip if you are born again. If you are not born again, you are still in his grip! But the good news is that you can get out of it. Jesus is the **way out**. He is also the way **to** God the Father. In fact, you can go straight from Satan to God through Jesus Christ. We must confess, renounce and repent of all our sins. We have to realise, acknowledge and understand that **we are sinners** – lost; that hell awaits us. One day we shall stand before the Lord Jesus Christ to answer for our lives and what we have done with them. Will He be your Judge or Saviour? You choose!

We had a man come to one of our meetings whom we will call Barry. He was the brother of a lady who is involved in the production of the colour films for the FGBMFI *Voice* magazine. She got her brother, a sick man with only a few weeks to live, along to one of our Power, Praise and Healing meetings. She had been born again and wanted to see him born again. He came and listened but at the end of it all he came to me and said, 'Well, I'm all right. I don't need to be born again. I don't need this Jesus of yours, because I've been a good guy. I've never done anybody any harm. I've always tried to help people. If somebody was in trouble, I'd try to help them. I'd have given my last penny away if it was needed. God has got to be good to me because I've been such a good chap.' I tried to point out to him that he was lost, damned and going to hell. That he was a sinner in God's sight. What he had done was, in God's sight, rubbish, filthy rags. But he would not have it. I prayed a simple prayer with him. I did not pray for salvation. But the prayer he didn't hear asked God to save him and bring him to his senses, as I knew he had not long to live.

Almost lost eternally

About a week after he went away, the Holy Spirit started working in him and he was telling people about the amazing meeting he had been to in South Norwood. How he had seen people healed and delivered – something he had never witnessed before. People were going down on the floor like ninepins. It was like a battlefield out the front. That is how it seems to be in the ministry time. God starts doing things. People are being healed and delivered and there are often manifestations of demonic oppression. Barry had seen all this and heard people testify to their deliverance or their healing from back pain, stiff joints, migraine, fears and other troubles. It really touched him, but he remained a lost sinner that night.

Once the Holy Spirit started to work in him, he told people he was going back to the next meeting that following month. 'I'm going to get there,' he said. By then he was not far from death's door, though he did not know it. He had cancer. He got to the meeting and listened. Then, when I made the salvation call, he was the first out to the front. He said the sinner's prayer and really meant it. He truly got born again. He just made it! That was about 9.30 pm. He died the same day. As they took him home in the car he said, 'I fancy a meal.' So they stopped the car at an Indian takeaway beside the road and took an Indian meal out to him. He started to eat as they went back to the shop for something. When they returned to the car he was dead. But **he made it!** He had been turned from the kingdom of darkness to the kingdom of light. That was good news to Barry – the best news he ever had. His reward is that he is going to be with Jesus for all eternity, just like us. This is the good news – for we are all sinners, lost before we know Jesus, because of our sin.

John tells us in his Gospel that as many as received Jesus were given the right to become the children of God – those who believe in His name, those who were born, not of blood, nor of the will of the flesh, nor of the will of man, but of God! Born of God. When we confess, renounce and repent and accept what Jesus has done for us on Calvary's Cross, make him our Lord and Saviour, admit we are sinners, **then** we can be born again. We have then appropriated our salvation. What He did was to shed His blood for us at Calvary, making atonement for our sins if we will accept it.

Chapter 3

Trotting Alongside
a Budding Evangelist

The meetings in that small church near Trafalgar Square in 1962 were to change our lives completely. We now wanted to follow the Lord Jesus but it was not easy. Few books were available about healing and deliverance and little about the experience of being 'born again', though we purchased a copy of T.L. Osborn's *Healing the Sick*, which was a great source of inspiration to us. I think this was in the Lord's plan though, for he led us back to the Bible. So it was that we learned about healing and deliverance from this unchanging source of information. It has saved us from many errors.

We read the verses in Matthew 7:21–23 and wondered. Some people said to us, 'These verses show that you must not cast out demons. If you do so, the Lord will say to you, *"I never knew you!"'* We then realised that these verses ended the Sermon on the Mount, in which the Lord Jesus instructed His disciples how to live. We learned that people who were eager to cast out demons but were not willing to accept the teaching of this Sermon as the guide to their lives were in great danger of being rejected by the Lord Jesus. That sobered us very much, for our lives fell far short of these requirements. We realised we had to pursue holiness. As young Christians, that seemed too much for us, but we were willing to allow the Holy Spirit to help us. And it is wonderful that the Lord Jesus accepts our willingness to do it almost as if we were doing it. All our bad habits – smoking, drinking, partying – had left us. We did not give them up, they seemed to give us up. So did many of our friends and acquaintances. They were not pleased with the changes that had taken place in our lives and left us. We did not mind, as we had found a real Friend in the Lord Jesus and many people, with whom we could share the joy of belonging to the Lord Jesus became our new friends.

In 1962 we lived in a semi-detached house in Hayes, Kent. T.L. Osborn's offices were in Birmingham in those days. They sent us some of their literature and offered us records of their crusades. We ordered a couple, one of which was *The Conquest of Jericho*. We enjoyed listening to the records. They greatly encouraged us. We met a lady in a local church who was very keen to hear this record, so we invited her along for an evening. She came and brought her daughter, about 20 years old. When we played the records the young daughter started to cry and we heard some odd noises, a kind of whining and whimpering. We were very puzzled and tried to comfort her. We asked the Lord Jesus to bless her and grant her His peace. But we remained puzzled.

We did not know then that people living in our civilised country could be troubled by demons. We had heard about demons being active in far away countries – T.L. Osborn encountered them in Africa – but not here. Then an evangelistic meeting was announced in Wimbledon with T.L. Osborn as the speaker. We went to hear him. When we arrived a great crowd was waiting for the doors to open, so we joined them. An air of expectancy was over us all. After an hour or so we were allowed into the hall and were glad to have a place towards the front.

I well remember the young boy who sat next to us with his father. As T.L. Osborn preached about the power of the Lord Jesus to heal, this young lad started to wipe his eyes, then cried and grasped his father's coat. There was some excited whispering between them. Then the father started to cry too. I looked at them and the father whispered to me, 'My son was blind, but now he can see!' It sounded right out of the New Testament and I was rejoicing deeply in my heart.

Tithing for today?

During that meeting T.L. Osborn also showed a film taken during one of his crusades. He explained that he hoped to supply many local missionaries with copies of his films – but he needed finance for trucks, projectors, generators, leaflets and copies of the films. Would some people please promise to give money for these things? He would not mind if somebody could only afford to pay by monthly instalments. John got up. We wanted to pay for a copy of a film for congregations in Africa. It meant paying £3 a month for 12 months. That was in 1963 or 1964 when £3 was worth the same as £30 today. It was not easy for us, but we gladly promised. This brought a great change to our finances. We had started to tithe as described in the Bible, and found the promise of blessing God gives to those who tithe very real indeed. We started to be truly blessed. We noticed the financial blessing very quickly. The spiritual blessing took us over many hurdles and through many battles, but the blessings were there and they grew.

We started to hire an Osborn film. I think it was called *Java Harvest*. We managed to find a believer who owned a projector and was willing to show the film. After the film John used to make a brief call for anybody who wanted to follow the Lord Jesus. There were often a few who accepted the Lord's offer. In one place I remember there was an elderly lady in a wheelchair, who suffered from arthritis. After the film she asked John to come and talk to her. Then she asked him to pray that she might be healed. Some days later we were told that she was seen shopping in the High Street – without the wheelchair and walking well for a lady of her age. What a wonderful encouragement!

At Maxwell-Whyte meetings

One day we met somebody who told us about meetings in London's Victoria Street. Demons were cast out by a man who had come from Canada. We were intrigued. We had to find out about this! So we went. Somehow the young lady who had whined and whimpered in our house was still in our minds. These meetings were very different from those we had attended near Trafalgar Square. This speaker commanded demons to leave people, who often fell to the floor. We witnessed some alarming manifestations – shrieking, screaming, coughing, burping and other queer noises. Some people lay still on the floor, others seemed to fight with unseen powers. We heard human voices shriek, 'Don't speak that Name!'; 'We were here first!' until there was a cough or another scream.

H. Maxwell-Whyte used to preach from the four Gospels. He explained the word translated 'healing' in our Bible is the Greek *sozo*, which means much more than healing. It includes complete deliverance from sin, sickness and evil spirits. One evening he specially talked about Dr Luke, the writer of the third Gospel. This well educated man accepted the miracles the Lord Jesus did – even to casting out a fever. The Lord spoke to the fever, and it obeyed and left. A demon had caused that fever. One can discern the wiles of Satan in this incident – a dozen weary men arriving for a meal and staying for a night – but the lady of the house is in bed with a fever!

Learning fast!

It was not long before we were involved in the meetings. At the end of the sermon Maxwell-Whyte prayed with people to receive salvation and healing. He started to pray for the sick, laying his hands on them and rebuking the sickness or evil spirit. The person usually fell slowly to the floor. John had been willing to serve as a steward but was then invited by Maxwell-Whyte to continue the ministry. So he found that demons obeyed him too, as he confronted them in the Name of the Lord Jesus. We saw many people get up off the floor, lift up their hands and say, 'I am healed, praise the Lord!'

There was usually a bookstall at these meetings, and we bought one or two books. One book did not seem right. It had come from America and we had doubts about this person's ministry. Then the Lord brought us a little booklet called *Expelling Demons*, by Derek Prince. We were very grateful for this booklet. It was so sane and scriptural and confirmed the things we had seen and heard.

The Lord Jesus had encouraged us to work in this ministry. We learned about the healing of broken hearts, confession, forgiveness – and above all to have patience. John and I were very ordinary business people. We enjoyed people's company, a good game of rummy, gardening and relaxing. This was all to change. We were called into a battle. It is still going on and we don't expect it to stop until the Lord Jesus returns.

A vicar in a church in South London was interested in showing his congregation an Osborn film. The church had been bombed during the war and was still partly derelict, but one side of the building had been restored and was used for services. The vicar was a very kind man, keen on the healing side of the ministry. The film was well received. I remember it ended with a picture of a poor old woman giving thanks to the Lord for giving her back her eyesight. Tears were rolling from her restored eyes. In that congregation was a young lady with curly ginger hair. Many people there talked to us but she turned her back and said some grumpy words to us over her shoulder. She clearly rejected us and the film – she did not like us. We knew then that demons were at work in her. Later on we learned that this young lady had been troubled all her life. Let us call her Ginger. She used to sit in the back pew of the church near some bookshelves, so she could hide. Sometimes she slithered onto the floor during a Communion Service, sometimes she got very angry and threw a Bible across the pews. Her hands used to be twisted. Some weeks later she still did not look at us. By then we had joined this church, where we had many blessed hours.

The church had a good youth group. Some youngsters had come to the coffee bar and wanted to join them. Some had asked to be baptised. I remember a baptismal service – in the modern version – when the candidates were asked to say a prayer of commitment to the Lord Jesus and renounce the devil and all his works. One young lady was in great difficulties. She could not say, 'I renounce the devil and all his works.' She had several tries: 'I renounce ... I renounce ...' then she swayed and froze. The vicar did not hesitate. He commanded the evil spirit to come out of the young lady – and with a shriek it went! She was then able to renounce the devil and all his works.

In the late 1960s Jean Darnall, an American lady preacher, had been invited by the vicar of a beautiful Wren church not far from St Paul's Cathedral to lead several healing meetings. John was delighted when he was asked to play the organ for the services. At the end of one service we were going home and passed a pew, where a lady with a mass of beautiful golden hair flung over the top of the pew was crying bitterly. We stopped and asked the Lord what to do. This meeting was not open for people to pray for others, so we just prayed a soft prayer in passing and went home.

A new house is needed

In 1968 we were looking for another house. We had prayed for a young lady and she had let out some loud screams. We were then living in a semi-detached, so we were bothered about the noise, wondering what the neighbours would think. It sounded as if somebody was being murdered! We realised we had to look for another house. It would have to be detached and more isolated. We visited many estate offices, without success. Then one day we spotted an advert in the *Evening News*: 'Detached 4-bedroom house for sale – off road.' That sounded interesting! We rang the number and were invited to inspect the property straight away. So we did, one February evening. But we were very disheartened by what we saw. The house and garden were rather neglected, and many urgent repairs were needed. We were doubtful and asked the Lord whether the house was for us. It did not look right. We also needed a rather high mortgage and at that time mortgages were not available, particularly large ones. We wondered. The lady who owned the house was very keen to sell it, as it had been on the market for well over a year. We very much needed a detached house and we could meet the price which was lower because of its poor condition, but we could not obtain a suitable mortgage. Did that mean that the Lord was saying 'No'? We gave up the idea. Then John felt that some power might be interested in our not purchasing that house. So one morning in November 1968 when John set off for his office in the Strand, as he passed a small park on his way to the Station, he was led to rebuke any evil power that was stopping us from obtaining a mortgage. He did it loudly, so certain powers could hear it. He then walked into his office and within a few minutes the phone rang. It was an insurance agent. John was glad to hear him say, 'You want a mortgage? Come into my office and you can have one.' So in January, 1969, we moved into our house in South Norwood, where the Lord Jesus has blessed us. Many believers have found counsel and deliverance there and unbelievers have experienced the love of the Lord Jesus and been born again.

We settled in and felt at home in the new place. Then a few weeks later we were invited to the house of some new friends to meet a lady who was in great trouble. When we entered the friend's house we saw a girl sitting in the lounge with the same beautiful hair as the lady we had met in the Wren church in Ludgate Hill. When we enquired, they said they had been there with her and she had been crying, for she was in very big trouble. We walked into the room to meet the lady. Seeing us, she rolled off the settee on to the floor, and there she stayed. We bound the spirit that had been manifesting. She woke up, sat up and moved slowly back on to the settee.

We tried to talk to her but she was very reluctant. She was in her early 30s, and was a patient in a nearby mental hospital. She had caused many problems, attacked a nurse, tried to set fire to the place twice, pulled down the pictures on the passage wall, painted all the screws she could set her hand on with nail varnish, and stamped with her bare feet on the rose bushes in the garden. Now she had attacked a nurse again. The hospital authority had challenged her: 'We had to put you into a padded cell. If you do this again, you will stay there for good!' So she had tried to find comfort with these dear people, who had taken her to Jean Darnall's meeting and had now contacted us.

As we now lived in a detached house, we felt we could invite Jane (not her real name) to come and see us for a time of counselling and prayer. She accepted reluctantly, but she came. Now we heard her story. She had been brought up in a very caring family and was much loved, rather lonely as a child. She was scared of other children and when she had to join them at school, she wanted to disappear, hoping to avoid mixing with them. She pretended to faint. She did this several times and found she was excused play and some work at school and was now the subject of much attention. That went well for a little while, until one day she felt a strange power coming over her, throwing her down. She could not move and her body started to twitch under this force. People at the school were very alarmed and called for the doctor. Jane was diagnosed as epileptic. She had also become destructive, attacking and destroying things.

Occult powers defeated

While we were talking, it was mentioned that her father was an expert in water divining. She also had this 'scientific' gift and they were very glad to have it. We explained to her that this was an occult manifestation, forbidden in the Bible. It was divination. 'Oh, no!' she said. 'It is a science. Nothing to do with the occult!' Jane had repented of many sins and had asked the Lord Jesus to come into her heart. Many demons of destruction, murder and witchcraft had been cast out. But she was not free and there were occasions when we took her to the church in South London that she slithered to the floor during the Communion Service. There were times when neither Ginger nor Jane were to be seen. They had disappeared onto the floor!

Jane refused to repent of a spirit of water divining. She came to see us several times and we had to tell her we could not help her any more. Then, at our last meeting, at midnight, she said, 'I can see that water divining is not right. I will repent of it now.' She then renounced her occult gift and with a scream the spirit left and she was free of it. We had spent many hours with her, praying for healing of childhood memories and her hours in mental hospitals, and guided her in prayers of repentance and forgiveness. Immediately after that last meeting she went through a three-day stretch of unconsciousness, when many more demons left her. She was later offered a training place in a hospital and succeeded in obtaining an SEN. She told the authorities her life story and they accepted that she had been delivered. She served in the nursing profession until she retired a couple of years ago.

Let us go back to our time in the church in South London. John had become a Lay Reader and there were some wonderful outreach evenings. But there was a problem: the vicar and John could not agree about the return of the Lord Jesus. We were sad to learn that the vicar believed that Satan was already bound and in the

Abyss and that we were reigning with Christ now. We could not accept this. Did we not experience Satan and his evil spirits free, troubling believers and breaking up churches and fellowships? Then who could say Satan was bound and in the Abyss?

The Lord supplies abundantly

After about ten years we left the church, with great regret and started to meet, after much pressure from others in our Bible Study group, in our lounge. Now John was free to preach about being born again, healing and deliverance and the return of the Lord Jesus. Some other friends from the Bible Study group joined us, as well as Ginger and her friend. The Fellowship, now called The Norwood Christian Fellowship, met for three years in our lounge, for three years in a hall in Croydon, then for three more in the church hall of a beautiful C of E church in Upper Norwood (by invitation of the vicar who left after three years and retired).

Then we returned to our lounge. An extension had been built on to it. This was another work of our Lord supplying our need. An elderly lady had joined us. She was very upright and lived in a small flat with one sizeable room and a second small one. She shared a bathroom and toilet. Part of her living room was a kitchen with a small sink. The Fellowship loved her and appreciated her faithfulness in attending, and her eagerness to know the Lord Jesus more and more. At one of our Weekends she gave her heart to the Lord. The Fellowship helped her to instal a gas fire, bought warm bedding and a cassette recorder. After being with us for a few years she had a heart attack and died. One of us had a vision at the moment of her death – of her spirit rejoicing to be free of her body, rising up to the Lord Jesus. She was 81.

This dear lady, whom we thought so very poor, had left a will. She left us enough money to build the extension to our lounge and to furnish it as well, something she had more than once suggested we should do. We know we shall meet her again one day when the Lord Jesus returns to snatch away His people from the earth. St Paul tells us in 1 Thessalonians 4:14 that He will bring with Him those who died in Him.

It is now over 32 years since we went forward at the church near Trafalgar Square – over 30 years of battle and great blessings. We have come to know Him and His power. To Him be all the glory!

Chapter 4

Miracle at the Kitchen Door

When Elsa and I were first married, we lived in an old house which had been converted into flats. The rooms were very large and freezing cold in the winter. It was somewhere to live, but we longed for a place of our own. Money was tight. I was working as a Print Buyer in an advertising agency and about a year after we took the flat a strike was declared in the printing industry.

One day a Master Printer I knew who had some very good connections phoned me to ask if I would be prepared to work the weekends in a factory on a Linotype machine. (I had earlier been in charge of a Linotype department.) I asked him about the pay and where the job would be. I could name my price, he said, and the job was in Hampshire. After a few moments' consideration, I named my hourly rate and said that if they agreed, it was a deal! Amazingly they did, for I had set quite a high figure to cover my travelling costs and lunches. I worked on Friday evenings, all day on the Saturdays and most of the Sundays for some six weeks. This enabled us to save enough for a deposit on a small house – all before I was born again!

We bought a small semi-detached house in Hayes,

Kent, a great jump ahead for us after the flat. But money was very tight – particularly as the demons of nicotine had to be satisfied! Still, we were very happy in our home and in 1962, while living there, we came to know the Lord Jesus – and the demons of nicotine went! Over the next few years we started finding ourselves with spare money each week. We were now tithing and the Lord Jesus was blessing us financially as well as spiritually. We often invited people to come and hear our records of sermons, mainly by T.L. Osborn, and also started to pray for troubled people. The very idea of people being troubled by demons was considered ridiculous and mediaeval in those days, so we had some dear people coming to see us and try to 'put us right'. Others wanted to know more about casting out demons.

The house in Hayes had a lovely outlook. There was a wood at the end of our long back garden with a huge oak tree by our bottom fence. The house had been built to an open plan with part of the back lounge doubling as a kitchen. The previous owners had had a wall built to separate the kitchen, though it could only be reached from the lounge or from the back door into the garden. We felt it was time this was improved, especially as we were blessed with more money. So we asked a reputable architect if we could build a kitchen outside the existing back door, to give us a bigger lounge for our expanding activities. He could see no problem getting planning permission, so we discussed our detailed requirements and he produced acceptable plans, which the local Council agreed. We then contacted a builder friend, agreed a price, and within a few weeks he started work.

The work proved to be a mountain – or an ocean? – of problems. First they dug a hole the size of our proposed kitchen outside our back door. To get into the garden and to the garage, we had to walk three planks, side by side, which swayed somewhat as we balanced on them. But we remained cheerful, thinking it would soon be over and we should be able to enjoy our new kitchen. Elsa and I made plans on graph paper where we would site the kitchen equipment, not knowing what was in store for us.

A few days later the builder came to us, looking troubled. Water was slowly seeping into the hole and he could not proceed with the work. We were then troubled too, with the beautiful view through the French doors to the wood and the old oak marred by a large heap of soil, some planks and a mucky hole in the foreground. The hole continued to fill, until it was about half full. We started enquiring as to the cause of this problem. A neighbour, who had lived nearby before the houses were built, told us that our house had been built on the site of a pond, which had been filled in before building began. A land drain had been put in to run into the wood at the end of the garden and the first manhole was on this land, which belonged to the local Council. Our builder got the Council's permission to rod the drain as far as the manhole, but the water remained. So the Council decided to rod their part of the land drain. Still the water remained!

Days became weeks and the water still stayed there. By now we had employed a solicitor, but this only yielded a sheaf of correspondence, a few meetings with Council officers in the wood and a large bill for us. Then the Council's surveyor came. He spent some time looking at the water in the hole, then told us we must get rid of the water or fill in the hole and forget about our new kitchen. How he expected the water to leave we did not know. He seemed to imply that we should forget the whole idea. The Council had done all they were going to do to clear the water, he said. It wasn't their problem anyway, but ours! Our builder friend was getting very fed up with the whole project and we were thoroughly disheartened. To make matters worse, we found there was water under the house too. The foundations were about 3ft deep and the water reached about half way up. The Council finally sent us a letter repeating what the surveyor had told us and left the ball firmly in our court.

We prayed about the problem, as we suspected something was stopping or wanted to stop us using our house more fully in the Lord's service. Every day the hole, the water and the planks faced us. What were we to do? Fill in the hole? Have a new land drain laid at considerable expense, leaving no money to build the kitchen? The whole situation was a grave disappointment, but we continued to pray and ask the Lord for help.

We then heard of a meeting to be held by Peter Scothern in Beckenham. We had come to know him a few years before and, having been greatly blessed by his ministry, we decided to go. It was a nice day and that evening we heard again that if we believed, the impossible would become possible, a word we felt was directed at us. Only a miracle could change our kitchen situation. That evening we had sung the chorus 'Expect a miracle when you pray'. So we drove home, put the car in the garage, but felt we could not go straight to bed. We stood at the back door staring down at the water and felt faith move in our hearts. Elsa said, 'Perhaps we should command the water to go?' We held hands and in a loud voice I said, 'Water, I command you in the Name of the Lord Jesus Christ, go away!' Faith filled my heart as I spoke. We then locked up and went to bed.

Next morning I was up at sunrise. I just had to get downstairs fast to see if anything had happened. I hoped the water had receded a bit, indicating that it would eventually go altogether. I longed to see this miracle. I unlocked the back door and stood on the step, then moved on to the planks. There was no water there! I shouted to Elsa, 'The water has gone!' She came rushing down and we stood looking at the hole together. All the water had gone and the ground was starting to dry out. The Lord had given us our miracle, and the 'mountain' (or 'ocean') had gone. We cried from joy, praising and thanking the Lord.

We now had to inform the Council. They sent their surveyor, who gave the impression he felt he had come on a fool's errand. He stood on the planks and looked at the hole, puzzled. He said only a few words. 'Well, I said that if the water went you could build your kitchen. The water has gone, so you can build it.' We got our kitchen and we also learned to trust the Lord Jesus totally, even when it involved removing water.

Chapter 5

The Basis of our Ministry

Blessings – Yes? Curses – No?

All the promises of God are 'Yes' and 'Amen' in Jesus Christ, according to 2 Corinthians 1:20. What then are God's promises about deliverance and healing? In Exodus 15:26 we find that Moses, acting as God's spokesman, says that if the Israelites will diligently heed the voice of the Lord their God and do what is right in His sight, give ear to His commandments and keep all His statutes, then none of the diseases which were brought upon the Egyptians would come upon them. Why? Because God says, *'I am the Lord who heals you.'* Again in Exodus 23:25 God promises His people that if they serve Him in the way He has laid down for them and not worship other gods, He will bless their bread and water. More than that, He declares, *'I will take sickness away from the midst of you.'* Obedience brings blessing with it, whereas disobedience leads to the curse of sickness among other things. We find this all spelt out in greater detail in Deuteronomy 28, 29 and 30. In Deuteronomy 28:1–14 we learn about all the blessings God will pour out on His people if they obey Him. More than this, they will overtake them! You cannot run away from God's blessing – even if you want to!

However, we need to be fully aware of what follows! You will see that from verse 15 onwards God spells out in detail what will follow disobedience to His Word. If we compare the curses with the blessings, we find that they start off with the same things in which God intended us to be blessed, and in the same order! These curses are followed by a host of others that will follow disobedience.

There is a further strong warning in verses 58–62 that the curses will follow on down the generations – what we call the Curse of the Law. We will examine this more closely in a later chapter. Suffice it to say that it is an area often overlooked by many when dealing with people troubled by evil spirits, to the detriment of those they are trying to help and set free. It is our experience that large numbers of Christians are under oppression because of the sinful practices of their ancestors.

The unchanging Christ

We find in Hebrews 13:8 that Jesus is always the same. He never changes, His purposes never change, His ways never change, His love never changes, His power never changes, nor does His authority. So what, then, was Jesus like? What did He do while He walked the earth? The only dependable source of information on this subject is the Word of God, the Bible. We read in Matthew 4:23, 24 that He went all round Galilee teaching in the synagogues, preaching the gospel of the kingdom of God. He healed all kinds of sickness and disease among the people – not only diseases of every kind, but also those who were tormented, the epileptics and the paralytics. That was what Jesus was like, and He never changes. He preached the Gospel of the kingdom of God, healed the sick and cast out demons or evil spirits

– the terms are synonymous. Matthew 9:35 carries the same message of Jesus' healing and deliverance ministry.

There was one man, we are told in Mark 1:40, who was not sure whether Jesus wanted to heal all those who were sick or diseased. He said to the Lord Jesus, *'If You are willing, You can make me clean.'* He was not sure if Jesus wanted to or was willing to. How often we find this today. People are not sure whether Jesus wants to heal them or set them free. Many times when we have asked them, 'Do you believe Jesus wants to heal you (or set you free)?' the response is 'I think so,' or 'I hope so.' We need to be certain. There has to be that inner certainty, because James warns us that doubters will receive nothing from the Lord. This could be one reason why some people are not healed.

Disease – a demon?

Another is that we sometimes pray the wrong prayer. If a demon needs to be cast out, it is not much good praying for healing. Jesus was always quite specific in His prayers for people. Those that needed healing He healed; those that needed an evil spirit or demon cast out received that kind of ministry. There was no confusion. Often a person will need a spirit cast out before they can be healed. Later, the fact that the demon has been cast out results in healing. We find a perfect example of this in Luke 13, where we read of a daughter of Abraham (that is a Jewess) who, Jesus said, had been bound by Satan for 18 years. He cast out the spirit of infirmity and she was immediately healed and could stand up straight. We have experienced the same thing. Individuals have come to us that have had great difficulty in standing up straight. But we have cast out the spirit of infirmity and they have been healed. Jesus loosed the woman from her infirmity and we are called upon to do the same.

There is an interesting story in Mark 1:23–26 which took place in the synagogue! Here we have a man who had presumably been going to the synagogue for many years but who had a demon. It might be appropriate here to remind ourselves that the Scriptures always refer to a person having a demon or evil spirit. We do not speak of a person being 'possessed' by a demon, though that is what most translations have. Rather the thought is that of something alongside or with a person. It is an important distinction, especially when we come to the vexed question of whether or not a Christian can be 'possessed'. We do not believe a Christian can be possessed by a demon, but we do believe that a great many Christians 'have' a demon (or evil spirit). It is quite evident, for example, where cancer is caused by a spirit, or where someone has been heavily into the occult and then gets born again. The demons do not leave when the person is born again – would that they did! No, the person will need deliverance ministry, the 'Bread of the Children' as Jesus called this ministry. It is an interesting fact that the early Church always carried out deliverance ministry on Gentile converts for some two years before they baptised them! Why? Because most, if not all of them had been into the occult in one form or another. Certainly they had worshipped false gods and, as the Scripture clearly states, behind every idol there is a demon (1 Corinthians 10:19, 20).

On one occasion we were invited to minister at an Anglican Church in South London during the time I was a licensed Lay Reader. The vicar had asked me to speak on occult involvement and how the deliverance ministry was God's way of setting His people free. The story of the man in the synagogue who had a demon came to life quite literally. There was a lady sitting quite near the front of the church, directly in line with the pulpit from which I was speaking. During my address I noticed that she was getting restless – the longer it went on, the more restless she became. After the service, the vicar and I went to the back of the church to shake hands with people as they left. Suddenly there was a piercing scream from the body of the church and one could hear chairs being thrown around. I recognised the scream – it was witchcraft. I said to the vicar, 'Come on!' We went to where a very small group of people were bending over someone on the floor who was screaming and thrashing around. It was the lady I had noticed earlier. I had known she had a problem – one did not need a word of knowledge to discern that! Immediately I started to command the evil spirit to come out of her. There were more screams accompanied by convulsions, then suddenly all was quiet.

It was noticeable that almost the entire congregation had retired to the back of the church at an early stage. I wonder if they had done the same in the synagogue when Jesus was there? She was free and the people had seen the word confirmed with signs following. However, such is the antagonism to this type of ministry in many churches, that we were never asked back again. For some reason people seem to fear this type of ministry, yet it is so dear to the heart of our Lord Jesus. He spent something like a third of His ministry casting out demons and setting the captives free. He also said that this was one of the signs that would follow believers. Where, one asks, are all the believers?

Deep needs met by Jesus

What was Jesus like? In Luke 7 we read the story of the

widow of Nain's son, a dead man being carried out for burial. Jesus' heart was touched with compassion for this poor woman, so He stopped the funeral procession. Then He said something which is often overlooked: *'Young man, I say to you, arise!'* The interesting point is that Jesus said, 'Young man'. Why? What is the significance of this? It is our belief that if Jesus had just said 'Arise!', **all** the dead would have arisen, for one day that is what will happen. It was the same with Jairus's daughter. Jesus said to her, *'Little girl, arise!'* And the same when he raised Lazarus from the dead. Jesus addressed the body directly, saying, *'Lazarus, come forth!'* Death is an enemy and Satan, our arch enemy, comes to steal, kill and destroy. But our Lord Jesus has come to destroy the work of the devil. He came to give us life, and life to the full.

On one occasion a man came to a meeting where I was speaking and asked if we would pray for his niece. We readily agreed, then asked what was wrong with the little girl. She had been involved in an accident and was so badly brain damaged that there was no hope of her living for more than a few days. Even if she did live, she would only be a vegetable for the rest of her life. The uncle wept and all our hearts at that meeting were touched with compassion for this little girl. We prayed and rebuked the spirit of death and asked the Lord Jesus to heal her. We heard later that she had made a remarkable recovery in a few days and that the healing continued. How we praised the Lord for this!

On another occasion, a lady came up to me at a church meeting where I was the speaker and asked if I would pray for her husband. Certainly, we told her, then asked what was wrong with him. 'He has cancer,' she said, 'with only a few weeks to live, according to the doctors.' She gave us a handkerchief which we then prayed over, rebuking the spirit of cancer in her husband. We felt the Holy Spirit insisting that she should take the handkerchief and put it under his pillow in the hospital bed. She agreed to do this when we told her. We heard no more at that time, but some 12 months later I was speaking at an FGBMFI Chapter Dinner when a man came up to me. 'John, you don't know me,' he said. 'We've never met and I've never spoken to you, but I want to thank you for praying for me.' 'Now hold on a minute,' I said. 'I don't know you, I've never met you and I've never spoken to you, yet I have prayed for you. How come?' 'Well,' he said, 'about 12 months ago you prayed over a handkerchief my wife brought to you and told her to put it under my pillow, as I only had a few weeks to live. I just wanted to say "Thank you" for praying for me.' This is what Jesus is like – raising up the seemingly or almost dead as well as the dead. And He does not change!

What did Jesus really say?

There is a story in John's gospel which is much misunderstood. The reason for this, I believe is that translators often have a great problem with the healing miracles of Jesus. We have become so conditioned by the errors we have been taught as fact, that when we come to the truth we cannot receive it. So we have to alter it slightly to fit in with our preconceived ideas of what God is like and what He wants to do. The passage in question is found in John 9:1–7 – the man born blind. How often we are blind to the truth of God's word through our traditions which we have received from men. It is a story often quoted to support the idea that God sends sickness or disease upon us, whereas in truth it is Satan who does this. What an affront to God this must be! God is the

One who wants to heal us and set us free, yet here we have men saying that it is God who has sent this sickness or disease upon a person.

There are also those who say that there must be some lesson which God wants you to learn through this so we cannot pray for you to be healed. The short answer to that is that the sooner you learn the lesson the better, for then you will be healed! What utter nonsense! The disciples ask the Lord Jesus a simple question, *'Who sinned, this man or his parents, that he was born blind?'* – a direct question. We would have to agree that there **are** people with sicknesses or diseases they have inherited from their forefathers because of the latter's occult practices. However, it is clear that this was not so here. We need to look closely at our Lord Jesus' reply, for it contains a fundamental truth, revealing who caused the man's blindness – and it was not his parents' sin nor his own sin. Note Jesus' reply to the disciples' question: *'Neither this man nor his parents sinned.'* Their question was answered!

Jesus could have left it at that and healed the man, but He appears to have wanted to elaborate so that we might understand God's workings more fully. Jesus tells His disciples that He must work the works of God and that those works would be revealed in the man. Perhaps if we give you the rendering of the passage it will become clear. Remember, there is no punctuation in the Greek. It is up to the translator's preference. So here is the J. L.-C. version of this passage:

> 'Neither this man nor his parents sinned. But so that the works of God should be revealed in him, I must work the works of Him who sent Me while it is day. The night is coming when no one can work. As long as I am in the world, I am the light of the world.'

This does no injustice to the wording at all and is, we feel, in keeping with the fact that God wants to heal all who are sick and deliver those who need deliverance. The work of God was to be displayed in this man's life by his being given his sight. This led to great opposition from the Pharisees. It is the same today. The Pharisees are still with us and just as blind today as they were then.

If we want to find out how Peter viewed the ministry of Jesus we need look no further than Acts 10:38:

> *'God anointed Jesus of Nazareth with the Holy Spirit and with power, who went about doing good and healing all who were oppressed by the devil, for God was with Him.'*

Part of Peter's address in the house of Cornelius at the end of which the Holy Spirit fell on the Gentiles present, as on the disciples in the beginning. That the Lord Jesus wants to continue this ministry is beyond question. If we believe He wants to save people, just as He did when He walked the earth and gave His life a ransom for us all, then it is only logical that He would also want to do good and heal all those who are oppressed by the devil today, because He does not change.

Therefore, go and do

What then was His disciples' ministry? In Matthew 10:1, 5–8 we read that He called the twelve to Him and gave them their instructions. Part of this reads:

> *'As you go, preach, saying, "The kingdom of heaven is at hand." Heal the sick, cleanse the lepers, raise*

54

the dead, cast out demons. Freely you have received, freely give.'

In Mark's account, in all probability gleaned first-hand from Peter, we see that the disciples went out and preached that people should repent. They cast out many demons, and anointed with oil many who were sick, and healed them. Firstly Jesus had shown them by example what to do, then He sent them out to do it themselves. It was the same with the seventy whom He sent out, we find. Jesus' words are recorded for us in Luke 10 where we again find that they are told to heal the sick in whatever city they enter and preach the gospel of the kingdom. When they came back they reported with joy that even the demons were subject to them in the name of their Lord Jesus! He then went on to tell them this very important thing:

'I give you the authority to trample on serpents and scorpions, and over all the power of the enemy, and nothing shall by any means hurt you.'

Theirs was the same ministry as that of the Twelve and of Jesus Himself. They had the same authority and power.

God never reveals everything all at once. Every revelation is followed at a later date by further revelation until we come to the end of the Bible, where we have the final revelation of God's plans for the world. There is a progression. So, too, in the healing and deliverance ministries. Firstly, it is Jesus alone who heals the sick and casts out demons; then it is the Twelve who are sent out to do the same things. This is followed by the Seventy being sent out, again to do the same things which Jesus Himself has done. Finally, in

Mark 16:15–18 we find the commission is given to every believer. This is underlined by the words of Jesus found in John 14:12:

> *'Most assuredly, I say to you, he who believes in Me, the works that I do he will do also; and greater works than these he will do, because I go to My Father.'*

There are also those who dispute the passage quoted in Mark's gospel, yet it appears in **almost all** MSS except Codex Sinaiticus and Codex Vaticanus. We are content to accept the majority of the Scriptures, rather than omit it because two MSS omit it! Further, our experience has proved the validity of this passage. And it still leaves the quotation in John to be explained away!

It is interesting that the beginning of our quotation from Mark states that the signs will follow believers. These signs are not apparent in many churches, so does that mean that they are full of unbelievers? Equally, where there is a church where the members believe in this commission of the Lord Jesus, we find the Lord Jesus confirming the word with signs following, just as we read in Mark 16:20! Our experience has shown that while many churches will accept the healing ministry, they will often not accept the ministry of deliverance. It is a stumbling block for them, almost, one feels, a rock of offence. Notice, too, that the ministry is for **all** believers not just a hierarchy – though we do accept that there are those who are called to this as a special ministry by the Lord Jesus. **He** is the One who ordains them, not men. Obviously we need power for this ministry – the power of the Holy Spirit. The only way to receive this power is through the Baptism of the Holy

Spirit. Well does Jesus admonish the disciples in Acts 1:7, telling them that they will receive power after the Holy Spirit has come upon them in the near future. They were already believers – but they had no power. In view of our Lord's statement the power they had received earlier to heal the sick and cast out demons would seem to have been temporary. After His ascension into heaven we find them hiding for fear of the Jewish authorities. Not much power in evidence now! Yet just 40 days later Peter and the others are out preaching repentance to the people without any semblance of fear whatever! What had happened? They received the promised power in the person of the descended Holy Spirit being poured out on them as Joel had prophesied and Jesus had promised.

Jesus is still doing it – for the same purpose: that the gospel might be preached with power and signs following. If the gospel is **not** being preached with signs following, the gospel is not being preached! Too many churches are so nice and orderly – 'all things decently and in order' – but don't come here to have demons cast out, for a Christian cannot have a demon! However, I do praise Jesus for the Anglican Church where I was a Lay Reader. We prayed for the sick every Sunday and if there was a demon to be cast out, we got on with it, whether the vicar was there or not. They could and did scream, lie on the floor – we did not mind, Jesus was at work setting the captives free. This was the church which Ginger attended and she has been set free by Jesus.

Not only will there be opposition from church people, but also from demons, who will endeavour to stop their victim from being set free or even saved. We have had folk say to us, 'I would like to believe and accept Jesus as my Lord and Saviour, but somehow I just can't.' We have taken authority over that spirit and commanded it to release the person to be free to decide. Usually the person's face has lit up or broken out in a smile and they have then made that decision and given their life to Jesus. On other occasions the demons will tell the person to leave the meeting. This happened a while back. A lady came to one of our monthly Power, Praise and Healing meetings who needed crutches to stand and walk. She had attended many hospitals and been seen by many specialists but they could not discover what was wrong with her, yet she could not walk. She had been brought by some friends, who came to me during the ministry time and asked me to go to where she was sitting, as she kept telling them she must go home. It was no use staying in the meeting, she said. The voices in her were telling her that Jesus was not alive, so let's go! This is no good!

After talking to her for a short while I realised that her real problem was the curse of the Law – occultism in her background. She was willing to confess, renounce and repent of all this as though it were her own iniquity and sin. She then commanded the spirits executing the curse in her life to leave and we cast them out. She had taken away from Satan the ground the evil spirits had had in her life, so they had to go – and go they did! The result was quite startling. When she had got outside the meeting place to go home, someone from the meeting saw her throw her crutches away and skip up the street! A few days later the lady herself rang me and told me the same story! Confirmation indeed! Mark wrote that these signs would follow those that believe.

The Scriptures are quite clear: we are called to preach the gospel of the Kingdom, and it will be with signs following. He has promised it and we believe it. Make John 14:12 a reality in your life and push back the powers of darkness. Cast them out of people's lives. We are called to the ministry of reconciliation and that must, of necessity, include casting out demons.

Chapter 6

The Danger of the Occult

The kingdom of satanic darkness

Anyone who seriously intends to take part in the ministry of setting the captives free must have a basic knowledge of the way the occult functions. While the occult is not responsible for all spiritual darkness, it is at the heart of a great deal of it and is a growing influence in our day. Every Christian, in fact, should be aware of the many traps and pitfalls the occult sets before the innocent and the unwary and the insidious ways it entices its victims into its clutches. You will then be able to avoid being trapped yourself and equipped to warn off many others – provided they will listen to you, for they still have God-given free will. Besides this, you also need to know how to deliver those who have already fallen into the clutches of the occult. Like anyone in the healing professions, you must be prepared for the two-fold ministry of prevention and cure.

The key Scripture that warns against dabbling in the occult is Deuteronomy 18:9–14, which sets out a complete list of occult practices:

> *'When you come into the land which the Lord your God is giving you, you shall not learn to follow the*

60

abominations of those nations. There shall not be found among you anyone who makes his son or his daughter pass through the fire, or one who practises witchcraft, or a soothsayer, or one who interprets omens, or a sorcerer, or one who conjures spells, or a medium, or a spiritist, or one who calls up the dead. For all who do these things are an abomination to the Lord, and because of these abominations the Lord your God drives them out from before you. You shall be blameless before the Lord your God. For these nations which you will dispossess listened to soothsayers and diviners. But as for you, the Lord your God has not appointed such for you.'

That reading lists all the various kinds of occult practices. Though some forms of contemporary occultism were unknown in Old Testament times, they can all be fitted quite comfortably under one of these broad headings. To enable you to understand these more readily, we have listed many of these practices in the Appendix. They are set down in alphabetical order for easy reference, but the list is not by any means exhaustive, so you will no doubt be able to think of others. Some of these practices seem pretty innocuous, while others are blatantly evil, but all at root are satanic.

People are induced to seek knowledge of things which God has not seen fit to reveal to us mainly from ignorance of His edicts and of the consequences of disobeying them. Others are determined to seek knowledge of the course of future events. Then there are those who seek to know what it is like after death, or who want to contact a departed loved one. All these practices are condemned by the word of God – and for good reason. Behind all these practices there lurks demonic power. So God, in His love for us, has forbidden us to contact the spirit world in any of these ways. The only contacts He wants us to have with the spirit world are firstly with Himself by means of His Holy Spirit, and secondly by taking authority over the situation of those we meet who are subjected by the occult and commanding those evil spirits to leave in the Name of Jesus.

But why should indulging in occult practices be so offensive to God? First of all, doing this is a direct affront to God Himself, since taking part in such practices involves our whole being and we begin to think that we can do without God's revelations and have no need to confess our sins. So we become self-sufficient and act as if we do not need God, instead of realising that we need to know God Himself in a personal relationship.

Then secondly God does not want us to indulge in these practices because we then lay ourselves wide open to oppression by demonic forces. If not dealt with, they will in time take over our whole being. There is then no other end in sight but the lake of fire (Revelation 20:15). This is the stark reality, as we have found during the course of our ministry. There is always a price to pay for allowing oneself to become subject to demonic powers – often the very sanity of the person concerned. The more one indulges in occult practices, the more he or she becomes alienated from God. As Isaiah rightly says:

'Your iniquities have separated you from your God; and your sins have hidden His face from you, so that He will not hear.' (Isaiah 59:2)

Sin and iniquity

At this point I must clear up a widely-held misunderstanding. Sin and iniquity are not just two different words for the same thing. There is a clear distinction between them, which needs to be understood by anyone in the deliverance ministry, for it is very important. We find God saying in Exodus:

> *'You shall have no other gods before Me. You shall not make for yourself any carved image, or any likeness of anything that is in heaven above, or that is in the earth beneath, or that is in the water under the earth. You shall not bow down to them nor serve them. For I, the Lord your God, am a jealous God, visiting the iniquity of the fathers on the children to the third and fourth generations of those who hate Me, but showing mercy to thousands, to those who love Me and keep My commandments.'*
>
> (Exodus 20:3–6)

Hating God and worshipping other gods He calls iniquity. When a person moves into the occult, he or she automatically sets up another god in place of the One True God. This god can range from the god of self at one end of the scale to Satan at the other, or anywhere in-between. Whatever the object of our worship, it is clearly labelled iniquity. Isaiah spoke of both iniquity and sin and two different words are used in Hebrew. Iniquity is *avon*, while Isaiah calls sin *chattath*. We find another word used for iniquity in the sense of vanity, namely *aven*. (There are other words translated as iniquity, but they are not extensively used and so do not affect this study.) The main Hebrew words used for sin are *chattath*, *chata* and *chet*. It is vital that we keep this distinction between sin and iniquity quite clear in our minds. Many of our modern Bible translations have obscured the difference and consequently many people are ignorant of what the Bible really says. For this reason we prefer to use the New King James or the Amplified Version, both of which translate these key words correctly.

We must also bear in mind that it is iniquity which brings punishment of some kind on up to four future generations, because of their forefathers' occult practices. We have met many people who are under the curse of the Law, as we call it, during our ministry. It will always show up by the fourth generation, if it has not done so earlier and then the cycle is repeated. That is how occult practices can continue in a family for several hundred years. They are passed on through the generations. The family has been opened up to harm by evil spirits. They are not out to help us, nor are they neutral. There is nothing benevolent about them. All they seek to do is to enslave us, because they are totally hostile to us. Seduction and deceit are their stock in trade, allied with treachery, with the sole object of misleading people and eventually destroying them.

Generational curses

There are many born-again believers who feel that when they accepted all that Jesus Christ has accomplished for them on the Cross, they were freed from the Law. They base this on an incorrect reading of Galatians 3:13 where we are told that Christ has redeemed us from the curse of the Law. What it actually says, of course, is that he has redeemed us from the *curse* of the Law – not Law! What then is this curse of the Law; are we under it if we are born-again, Spirit-filled believers? What would be the signs to look for in a person's life which would indicate that a curse is working and is there any scriptural basis for saying that such a curse can and does come down the generations? To answer these questions it might be helpful to first ask ourselves a few questions about blessings and whether these can come down the family line.

In Genesis 12:2, 3, God said to Abraham that He would bless those who blessed Abraham and curse those who cursed him; that all the families of the world would be blessed through him. Can we partake of the blessings spoken of here? Certainly we can as we read in Galatians 3:14. A similar thought is expressed in Genesis 18:18 where God declares that all the nations on earth will be blessed through Abraham. Surely we must be included in this for it clearly says **all** the nations on earth. These blessings have, of necessity, to come down the family line from Abraham.

In Psalm 1 we find that the one who delights in the Law of the Lord shall prosper in all he does and we find that this blessing is for us Gentiles if we meet the condition for the giving of the blessing. Isaiah tells us that the Lord Jesus will be given as a light to the Gentiles and that is a blessing beyond compare for us which we gladly accept. The Psalmist also says in Psalm 103 that God is the One who heals all our diseases and forgives all our sins and there is no question that we would most certainly attest to the truth of that statement. A similar thought is contained in Psalm 107:20 which declares that God sent forth His word and healed them, and another Psalm tells us that the Law of the Lord is perfect, converting the soul.

Isaiah is bold to declare that no weapon formed against the servants of the Lord will prevail and that we should condemn every tongue that speaks against us. This we have proved to be true in our experience as no doubt many others have. We would rightly claim that all these promises are for us and if that is so, then why is it thought unreasonable for the curses to be also for us? We find both in the Old Testament so it is no good claiming that they only applied before the Cross, as some do.

Freed from *all* Law?

When questioned as to the greatest commandment of all, Jesus replied,

> *'You shall love the Lord your God with all your heart, with all your soul, and with all your mind. This is the first and great commandment. And the second is like it: You shall love your neighbour as yourself. On these two commandments hang **all** the Law and the Prophets.'*   (Matthew 22:37–40)

There is no doubt in my mind that we would all agree that we should keep these two commandments. But it does not end there. Jesus, you will notice, said that on these two commandments hang **all** the Law and the Prophets. What did He want us to understand by this? We are to realise that, whilst we are not under the ceremonial Law, we are under the moral and spiritual laws of God as set out for us in His word. Paul says in 1 Corinthians 7:19:

> *'Circumcision is nothing and uncircumcision is nothing, but keeping the commandments of God is what matters.'*

It is obvious that if we do not keep God's commandments then we are lawless. There must be laws of God and they are necessary in order to reveal to us that we are sinners. Were there no commandments then there would be no sin. You cannot break a law which does not exist! Have we, then, kept even these first two commandments of God which Jesus quoted? Regretfully, we would have to say, 'No'. Who truly loves the Lord their God with all their heart, soul and mind and their neighbour as themselves?

We see then, that there are commandments of God we are required to keep. But this then begs the question of whether or not we come under any curses for failing to keep them and is it possible that we may come under a curse because our forefathers have failed to keep His commandments? To answer these questions we must go back to the word of God. In Deuteronomy 11:26–28 Moses sets before the people a blessing and a curse. There is a blessing promised for obedience to God's commands and a curse for disobedience. What he is saying is, if you want the blessings of God, keep His commandments else you will come under His curses. If we turn to Deuteronomy 28 we find that blessings are spelt out for keeping God's commandments and that it is not possible to run away from the blessings (who would want to, anyway?) – they will overtake you! These are all covered in verses 1–14. When we come to verse 15, however, we find that Moses starts to spell out the curses which will come upon the Children of God for disobedience – and again you cannot run away from them for they will also overtake you! Firstly, those following verses link the curse to the same things which in verses 1–14 were to have a blessing following them; and they are given in a similar order. Then we find a whole series of curses of just about every kind imaginable. And just to emphasise the point, as it were, Moses declares that:

> 'Every sickness and every plague, which is not written in the book of this law, will the Lord bring upon you until you are destroyed.'

Even more curses are contained in Deuteronomy 29 and 30.

Curses operating today

When the Children of Israel were about to go into the Promised Land, Moses gave them express instructions which we find set out in Deuteronomy 27. They were to build an altar on Mount Ebal when they had crossed over the Jordan and there they were to offer peace offerings and burnt offerings. An altar always speaks of sacrifice. This Mount Ebal was to be the mount on which curses would be spoken against those who did not keep the Law of God – His commandments – whilst Mount Gerazim was to be the Mount of blessing. Sacrifice was necessary to deal with the curses. Violation of the commandments of God would bring a curse into the life of the one committing the offence and also on their family as is evident from Deuteronomy 28:32 which speaks of the children being taken away captive because of what the parents have done; and verse 46 of the same chapter says:

> '*They* (the curses) *shall be upon you ... and on your descendants...*'

That we are all under a curse is obvious for we all die – death was a curse spoken by God in the Garden of Eden to Adam and in him we all die (1 Corinthians 15:22). Thus we see the principle of a curse coming down the generations established there in the beginning. The curse came because of disobedience some 6,000 years ago, and it is still with us, for all die. The consequence of disobedience was death. The breaking of God's commandments always has a price and the effects

68

of the curse let into a family will come down for up to four generations. In Deuteronomy 6:4, 5 is contained the first and great commandment quoted by the Lord Jesus. After quoting this He added that we are to love our neighbour as ourselves and said that all the Law and the Prophets hang on these two commands. Thus we see that **all** the Law, not just these two commandments, is included. We are to keep it **all**. Now in the verses in Exodus 20 we see that we are to have no other gods, nor images, nor idols nor the likeness of anything in the heavens above, the earth beneath, or in the waters; we are not to bow down to them nor worship them. Why?

> 'For I, the Lord your God, am a jealous God, visiting the iniquity of the fathers on the children to the third and fourth generations of those who hate Me, but showing mercy to thousands, to those who love Me and keep my commandments.'

Having any other god, bowing down to it or worshipping it in any way, God calls iniquity. (We dealt with the difference between iniquity and sin earlier in this chapter, as well as the question of children suffering because of their fathers' sin.)

One girl from Finland who attended many of our meetings admitted to being a witch. She heard the Gospel more than once, but always seemed closed to its claims. One evening, after my message, she came forward and grabbed hold of me round the waist with both arms locked behind my back. In the natural it should have been easy for her to throw me off balance, but I was quietly praying, as were other people present there. She pushed and tugged and struggled but, as the onlookers said afterwards, it seemed that I was like a rock that she could not move. After a few minutes she gave up the unequal contest and stood back panting and sweating with the exertion and cried, 'I **hate** you!' We assured her of God's love for her and once again invited her to repent of all her witchcraft, through which, on her own admission, she had sent more than one person to their death. But she would not accept the claim of the Lord Jesus on her life. Sad to relate, she threw herself out of a third-floor window a few weeks later and was killed. She had not realised that the demons always exact a price for failure, and also that you cannot attack a servant of God and get away with it. You lay yourself open to demonic forces, because God withdraws the protection He has exercised over you. If she had confessed, renounced and repented, she would no doubt have been set free of those demonic forces to which she was in bondage.

Practical help in Jesus

On another occasion we were introduced to a spiritist medium, a lady in her mid-forties, a pleasant person who held a very good position in the Civil Service. She asked for ministry as she wanted to give up her occult practices because she felt they were the cause of her mental problems – which they all too often are. At that time we were meeting with a small house group near Crystal Palace. We arranged that the lady would come to the house where we were meeting one Saturday afternoon, so that a small team of four could pray for her. Before starting the ministry, we all had a cup of tea in the kitchen, which was set on a lower level than the main hall, which was reached by a short flight of about four stairs. We vividly remember her, having drunk her tea, proceeding to the front room where the ministry was to take place up the stairs on all fours, barking like a dog! We finally managed to get her on a chair and commenced with a prayer of repentance. After this, we started commanding the mediumistic evil spirits to leave her.

It is vital for the person genuinely to confess, renounce and repent of what they have been into. We use a prayer something like this: 'Holy Father in heaven, I come to you in Jesus' Name, and I confess, renounce and repent of every occult practice I and my forefathers back to the fourth generation have been into. I claim the blood of Jesus to cleanse me and set me free. Satan, I renounce you and all your works. In the Name of Jesus I command every spirit of _____ (here they should name the practices they have been into, plus any occult involvements their mothers and fathers and other forefathers have been into that they are aware of) and every spirit executing the curse of the Law to leave me now.' The spirit(s) should then be commanded to leave in the Name of Jesus.

Those who are ministering should expect there to be some manifestat;on, such as heavy breathing, spitting, coughing, screaming or vomiting something which needs to come out through the mouth. A bowl can be useful! Do not be deceived into thinking that all the spirits will go at once. That seldom happens. More often than not, particularly with occult spirits, there are several of the same type. They seem to go in families. Rely on the Holy Spirit. Your own understanding can often lead you down wrong paths. Ask for the Holy Spirit to come upon the person you are praying for. Pray in tongues if He leads you that way. This will often produce a breakthrough.

Our spiritist medium was set free after quite a struggle and not without vomiting and screaming. After that was over, we asked for her to be filled afresh with the Holy Spirit. This is vital. Remember, Jesus told of a spirit

71

coming out of a person and going through the dry places of the earth, seeking rest but finding none. He then added this warning: The spirit thought to itself it would go back to the 'home' it had come from and did so, finding it swept clean and **empty**. So make sure that all the areas of the personality of the person you have been praying for are fully given to the Lord Jesus and His Spirit.

Even the furniture was infested

There was a sequel to our lady's deliverance. She found that all her furniture was infested and so there was no peace in her home. In the end she took it all into the garden and burnt it. She assured us this was the only remedy. We were not surprised. Never forget that things can be demonised as well as people. That is why we need to be careful what we bring into our homes.

Some people consider playing with a ouija board or taking part in a seance all harmless fun. Many have told us that they only did it for a bit of fun. 'I don't really believe in all that nonsense.' Well, if you put your hand in the fire you should not be surprised if you get burnt! There have also been those who said, 'Well, I wanted to find out for myself what went on. From a purely Christian viewpoint, you understand.' You will come away needing deliverance ministry if you do, that's for sure.

So what are the most common signs that people have been into the occult or are suffering because of their fore-fathers' occult practices? Depression and migraines are perhaps the most common symptoms. This is not to say that everyone who suffers from depression or migraines has been into the occult, but it is often so. Fits of temper and rage can also result from demonic oppression, as do fears of every kind, nightmares and blasphemous and suicidal thoughts. Pornography and sexual perversions are not infrequently initiated by occult subjection too.

Look for an occult link in the background where there is a history of a certain kind of illness in a family repeated from one generation to the next. A succession of accidents may afflict a family, as can financial hardship, despite there being plenty of money coming in. A family with a history of family breakdowns has probably been into the occult. This also applies to families where success in everyday life always seems to just elude them. Father was going to be promoted, but then for no obvious reason the Board changed their mind and gave the job to someone else. This scenario is repeated again and again. It becomes the story of their life.

A common problem – misinterpreting Scripture

Another misunderstanding we need to clear up is the vexed question of whether we really suffer because of our forefathers' occult practices. Ezekiel 18 could encourage us to believe that only the one committing such acts will suffer. We read in Ezekiel 18:4 that *'The soul who sins shall die.'* The following verses declare that if a man does what is right and just, keeping the statutes and judgements of God faithfully, he shall live. Then we read that if such a man has a son who does not follow after the commandments of God, he shall die – *'his blood shall be upon him.'* Ezekiel then goes a stage further and says that if such a son shall himself have a son who sees all the evil his father has done but, like his grandfather, keeps to God's ordinances, he shall live, while his father shall die. Verse 20 records that,

*'The soul who sins shall die. The son shall not bear the **guilt** of the father, nor the father bear the guilt of*

73

the son. The righteousness of the righteous shall be upon himself and the wickedness of the wicked shall be upon himself.'

It is important to realise that it is the **guilt** that will not be imputed to the son and with it not the penalty either, which was death. That is why it says it is the soul that sins shall die. If we stop a moment and consider the whole situation, it should become clear how God can visit the iniquity of a father on his children to the third and fourth generation, yet not contradict Himself. To give a specific example, consider a murderer who in those days would have forfeited his life for his deed. After the sentence had been carried out, his entire family would obviously have suffered as a result. They would probably have suffered severe poverty, for there was no Welfare State then. They would also have been ostracised as undesirable in view of what their father had done and would never have lived it down. Now apply that to what God says to us in Ezekiel's writing. The father goes into occult practices and is oppressed by an evil spirit, which now enters his whole family through him. Even after he dies, his children, already oppressed by evil forces, are still subject to those forces. But at the same time they do not pay the **penalty** for their father's misdeeds, which is death. So there is no contradiction in the Word of God.

It can be helpful to get someone who has been into the occult, or whose ancestors have, to ask a few pertinent questions. These need not be exhaustive but could help you clear the way for setting that person free of the forces oppressing them. They will need to confess, renounce and repent of each sin as they become aware of it. In this way they can take away from Satan all the ground he has claimed in their lives. Then the spirits must go. People with an occult background are usually indifferent to spiritual things such as reading the Bible, prayer and attending church meetings. They tend to hold on to unscriptural beliefs and could find it difficult or even impossible to take Communion. They must be willing to destroy any and every occult object they possess, no matter what its value. If they do not, an open door will remain for the powers of darkness to gain a new foothold in their life.

We had one young lady who had a crystal ball at home. She promised to bring it to the church where we had been ministering and give it to the Pastor to dispose of. He had undertaken to smash it with a hammer. When he endeavoured to do this, it had little effect. In the end, they took the ball out to sea in a boat and threw it over the side into deep water!

Role-playing – a game?

Any man who has come out of an involvement with the Freemasons must burn all his books and regalia. He could find it difficult to burn some of them as they seem to refuse to burn. Nevertheless they must all go if he is to gain total freedom. As a last resort there is always the dustbin! Some years ago, after we had spoken at an FGBMFI teaching day, we received a letter from one of the men who attended. This is an extract from it:

'Following a teaching day led by John Linden-Cook, I thought you would be interested to hear what happened to me at that meeting. I had been involved in reading pornographic literature and fantasy and science fiction books. I had also been involved in playing fantasy role-playing games, like Dungeons and Dragons and Advanced Dungeons and Dragons and similar games involving mythical gods, for 10 years. But I was not aware that I was under a curse from these influences. (Freemasonry is a role-playing activity.) I had stopped reading pornographic books when I became a Christian two years ago, but it came as a shock to realise that I was under bondage to sexual oppression. Through John's ministry on the Saturday morning, I became aware of my problems and was released from the curse of the Law. Over the next two weeks I lost all interest in fantasy role-playing games and felt an inner compulsion to get rid of all my books and games as John had told me to do. I did so one afternoon in a glorious conflagration. This brought me a tremendous spiritual release and exposed the sexual oppression I had been under. I had been a homosexual and paedophile since early childhood. But now I am free, praise the Lord!'

You may find when counselling and praying with someone who has been deeply into these practices, that they have difficulty in saying the prayer of confession and renunciation. This is quite common, but can easily be dealt with in the following way: Take authority in the Name of Jesus and bind the spirit that is stopping the person from confessing and release them, so they are free to do so. It may be necessary to do this more than once during their confession and renunciation, as the spirits will do all they can to stop the confession. The reason for this is obvious. Once confession has taken place the ground in the person's life on which the evil spirit(s) were sitting is taken away and they know that they will have to leave.

If, as we do, you take Communion before ministering privately to someone who has been into the occult, you may find it necessary to bind the spirit who will endeavour to stop them from taking the Communion, especially the wine, the symbol of our Saviour's blood, by which we overcome Satan. (We have now given up private ministry, as so many people now ask for ministry, it is no longer practicable.)

It could prove helpful to demand the name of the ruling spirit operating in the person's life. If you embark on this course, do not give up until you know in your spirit that you have been given its **true** name, not a false one. Don't believe everything they tell you – they are inveterate liars! Quote the word of God against them – the results can prove very interesting! This is why it is important for us to know the Scriptures, particularly those relating to deliverance ministry. There are plenty of them.

Never let these spirits frighten you by their boasts that they will kill the person before they go. On the other hand, you should be aware that they may try to get someone who has been deep in the occult to strangle themselves. Never rely on your own powers or resources but always look to the Lord Jesus to see you through the battle. Call upon Him and claim the protection of the Blood of Jesus, then take the battle into the enemy's camp. Remember, **we have the victory!**

Chapter 7

The Pendulum Swinger

'It was a custom of mine to walk away my "blues", and twice a week I did a regular stint of 12 miles enjoying the exercise and the fresh air, but on this occasion my legs were troubling me. My veins were throbbing, and the soles of my feet were red hot as I limped painfully along the High Street, just longing to get home, and soak my feet in cold water. I was in no mood for conversation, but when my friendly neighbour asked me what the trouble was, I gave a lame excuse and didn't linger. I was greatly surprised when she called that evening with her husband and treatment for my swollen veins: crepe bandages, magnesium sulphate paste, flowers, a cake and a deep concern for my well-being. We spent a long time in conversation and I soon discovered that she was a committed Christian. I admitted that I didn't attend a church because the gospel as preached by so many churches today seemed so irrelevant to present-day needs, and I mentioned my interest in the occult.

This information horrified her, as she asked me if I realised what I was doing was an abomination to God. Quoting passages from the Bible (1 John 4:1) which greatly impressed me, but at the same time I couldn't see anything wrong in what I was doing. So far as I was concerned I was amusing myself with a pendulum and some divining rods, tapping vibrations, without any evil intent, but little realising that I was being used by demonic forces, and getting deeper into bondage. My promise to read the Bible didn't do anything for me because of my interest in the occult which blinded my eyes to the truth.

A burden lifted

When a visit to the Norwood Christian Fellowship was mentioned I went along to one of their monthly Deliverance and Healing meetings and was greatly impressed with the word that was given. To see people being laid low by the power of the Holy Spirit I thought, was dubious; it had no effect on me when I went forward. But despite my reservations I went to the next meeting, and this time I was laid low as John commanded the evil spirits to leave me and I couldn't rise from the floor. Great gusts of air seemed to come from my stomach as the demons were expelled from me and when I got to my feet I felt as though a burden had been lifted from me.

Very gratifying, but more so, when later I picked up my Bible and found that whereas before I couldn't make sense of the archaic phrases, now the printed word had become the Living Word, and the Bible has now become my daily reading as my eyes were opened, and it was indeed a revelation of the love of God.

Such, however, was the nature of my self-will that I was still undecided about the use of the pendulum and found it hard to accept that something I had used as a plaything was evil; the only way to find out was to ask the Lord Jesus. With outstretched arm I used the pendulum, got it spinning at speed, stopped it, and then asked the Lord Jesus that if this thing was evil to give me a sign. The sign was immediate!

As I tried to use the pendulum again it was motionless and remained that way despite my efforts to get it going. I was overwhelmed as I sank to my knees in fervent prayer and thankfulness. All the doubts, fears and uncertainties were swept away in the silence; and this, together with my freedom from bondage has turned my life around. Divining rods, books and pendulum were dumped into the wheeley bin.

I didn't realise at the time of my release from bondage that Satan does not give in easily. My dabbling with the occult included seances, the pendulum, divination and the ouija board, which is no mere game, and led me deeper into the toils of the devil. In the space of about 10 nights my sleep was disturbed by frightening visitations from demonic spirits in various forms; sprites, pixies, elves with ugly threatening leering faces. All this brought about by my ignorance of the spiritual warfare being waged between the forces of evil and the power of God. The fact that I was so speedily released I can ascribe to the ministry of John and Elsa and other members of the Norwood Christian Fellowship and many other friends upholding me in prayer. It was something I could never have attempted in my own power. So there I was at the age of 84, with all my male relations and friends having departed, and feeling like the last of the Mohicans and a "has been" being given a new lease of life which I have accepted gratefully.

Attendance at the Fellowship and Bible Study Group was essential as I have a lot of leeway to make up, and I would urge anyone who feels "past it" to take up the challenge. The life of the Spirit is never dull, drear, dead or dry, and I shall be going to High Leigh again this year to renew acquaintance with some delightful Christians.

My progress hasn't been all sweetness and light; I am still troubled at times by my self-will, and now and again the voice of the Tempter is heard. But now I can say with conviction, "Blessed assurance, Jesus is mine". Blessed by the knowledge of God's power to change people's lives, I look forward to a new life with listening faith.'

Chapter 8

Divorce Threat Vanishes Instantly

'Several years ago our lives were completely transformed. More recently my wife Mary and I agreed to go on a touring holiday round Scotland. We started north in torrential rain, but it cleared after a while and we arrived early in Penrith, so we decided to divert and enjoy the beauties of Ullswater. It was mild for early April and everything looked fresh and magical. We quickly became aware that God was with us and wanted to take us on a conducted tour of His creation. He went on to bless us all the way round Scotland and our last stretch of driving there proved to be one of the most beautiful evenings I have ever spent in a car.

But it has not always been like this. Twenty years ago Mary was on the point of divorcing me – and I do not blame her. She had manfully struggled to raise our two boys. She gave me no illusions that when they were off her hands, then out I went! I had tried to love her, indeed I was very fond of her and the two boys, but somehow my affection never came out the way I intended, and was certainly not to their liking. Try as I might, all I gave Mary was hell. Years later she told me that I had even tried to murder her – twice!

A "chance" acquaintance had invited Mary to a

prayer meeting on one Saturday night in February 1967. She preferred to stay at home with the boys, so she "volunteered" me, reasoning that it couldn't do me much harm, even if it did me little good. Anyway it would get me out of her hair for the evening. I knew the hostess by sight and as I entered the room – have you ever felt you were not wanted? All the chairs were occupied by strangers to me with the exception of my hostess. In the end it was suggested that I could sit on the coal scuttle in the fireplace.

A young man named John began sharing the Gospel, the good news about Jesus. He was describing – well, "miracles" is the only word I can use. What he was saying was exactly what I had been seeking all my life. I listened enthralled and when I reached home I was bursting to tell Mary. She was asleep or playing doggo, so I went to bed.

As soon as my ear touched the pillow the Lord said, "You've got to see that man again!" "That is a good idea," I responded. I would have to find out his full name and look out for him. As I turned on to the other ear the Lord repeated, "You've got to see that man again!" "Yes, Lord I agree." When I rolled over again the Lord repeated what He had said once more.

Sleep denied

By about 3 am I realised first, that I had to see John whatever-his-name-was again, and second, the Lord was going to make sure I did by not allowing me a wink of sleep all night. After sundry traumas I spoke to John on the 'phone and arranged to see him on my way out to play the organ at a country church some miles outside Ipswich. John, I gathered, had to return fairly sharpish to London to a service in his usual church.

As soon as John answered my knock, he asked me where I lived. My address was out of my mouth before I could think. To my horror he said that he and his wife would come up to see us that very afternoon. Now this was just not on! I had a good idea how Mary would react, so I tried to tell John that his services were needed in London or elsewhere, but definitely not in my home. All to no avail. For whatever reasons, his mind was made up that he was coming to visit me at my home that afternoon.

In my efforts to find Jesus I had wandered into a number of sects, but so far to no avail. Mary had put up with the different people's comings and goings all this time but I knew her tolerance was wearing thin.

Thus it was with a sense of foreboding I left to reach the church in time for the service. Returning home, I had my lunch which Mary had prepared and then told her about our two visitors. As anticipated, Mary was definite. They were my guests and I could look after them. If they would like tea then I could fix it. She was not coming to see them and was definite now, that divorce proceedings would be started the next day! In the middle of this domestic confrontation, they arrived.

We were living in a fairly large bungalow at this time, so there was plenty of room for Mary and our younger son to make themselves scarce. Our elder son was up at Cambridge. This allowed my two visitors and me to go into a sitting room on our own. I wasn't very happy nor clear about what was happening. It was somehow out of my hands. I can remember little of what took place until just before they left, when John asked me if I were baptised. Of course I was, I had been "done" as a baby then carried on as a lifelong Anglican. Surprisingly he told me to sit down – in one of my own chairs – and proceeded to put his hands on my head and said, "Receive the Holy Spirit!" or something like that. He then told me to say something even if it were only "Thank you".

This I did. I'd always been taught to be grateful, but blowed if I knew whom I was thanking or for what. Both seemed pleased with the afternoon's session and indicated their desire to leave for London. They left me somewhat bemused.

I just didn't know what to make of things. The sky seemed strangely bluer and the grass greener. Then I saw our younger son. He was in his mid-teens and seemed to delight in being as scruffy as he dared – but now he was beautiful. A few minutes later Mary came up to me and said, "If you stay changed as you are, I won't divorce you!"

True married bliss at last!

When I discussed this with Mary she thought it was some while later. She is probably correct, for it took some while for me to come to any degree of awareness. As the days went by, the wife I had always loved was more adorable than ever, lovable beyond my wildest dreams. Lovely as she was, she was still my wife and it was glorious that now when I tried to convey my love for her she accepted and responded in a way that had never happened before.

What was the change that had taken place in me? It took days, weeks, possibly a year or two, to comprehend what had taken place that Sunday afternoon. I began to appreciate the truth. I had been demon-possessed and now I had been delivered, I was free! Freed from the demons of spiritualism (spiritism) and Freemasonry by the authority of the Name of Jesus! Mary told me, without any rancour, that living with me for the previous 16 or 17 years had been hell for her and the children. A few years later Mary herself was born again in the Holy Spirit and anointed with power from on high, praise the Lord! But that is her testimony.

It is hardly surprising that over the years we four have become exceedingly good friends. Although I have never asked John or Elsa Linden-Cook for details of what I now realise was a time of deliverance from evil spirits, comments have cropped up in the course of conversation. For example, I have always had a powerful grip, but Elsa commented quite recently that John had had the imprint of my fingers on his forearms for three weeks after I had gripped him through his jacket sleeves. John himself added that he thought both bones in both arms were going to be broken. I say this to make the point that however mighty Satan and his demons are, the name of Jesus is all-powerful to deal with every situation we are in, provided we are in the Father's will.

I will mention one other happening. During the spiritual warfare Elsa noticed a spot of blood had appeared upon the top of my head. (My parting is rather wide.) Neither she nor John had ever seen this before, nor since, I gather. What it was I do not know.

Now it was all over – but not quite. There were two other problems still to be resolved. Some three years after my major deliverance, while repeating some of the yoga asanas or exercises, I suddenly realised its occult nature. I immediately repented of it, renounced it and burnt all the literature I had on the subject. As the flames rose I experienced a sense of freedom and peace, a burden being lifted from me. This was the only occasion I experienced anything like this. As a matter of interest this revelation was given to me when I was performing the "Salute to the Sun". Here was I, a child of God the Father, the Creator, bowing down to part of His creation, which Scripture forbids.

A Christian conference? – No way!

About this time John tried to inveigle me into taking Mary to a Christian conference. As far as I was concerned this was not on. Spending part of one's holidays at a conference centre in the company of "religious nuts" walking round with Bibles under their arms was not my idea of a vacation. In the end John won, rather astutely. He asked me one day if I would take his mother up from Ipswich to see him, as he was somewhat busy. Readily I agreed, after all that we had come to mean to each other. When I asked him for his new address he replied that wasn't necessary. Would I bring her to the London Healing Mission's Healing Advance at High Leigh, Hoddesdon, Herts. Now I was getting into deep waters. How could I take John's mother to a conference and turn round and drive away? I decided that I just could not do it, so I asked John if he would book places for Mary and me. His reply? "I have already done so!" That's faith!

Whether a Healing Advance has the edge over an ecclesiastical retreat, I couldn't say, but I certainly learned a great deal during the week of the conference. The first missioner I met was the late Rev. Roy Jeremiah. Under his guidance I learned about spiritual gifts. At a service of blessing on the Thursday afternoon, Mary was born again of the Holy Spirit and anointed with the power from on high. She celebrated this by singing the last hymn in tongues. This, I thought, meant that I needed to have the gift of interpretation so that I could find out what she was up to. He explained the problem of my naivety and soon I was exercising the same gift as Mary, though it was six months before I reached her degree of fluency. Now I really had a new wife!

We continued to attend these summer meetings for some ten years until the then missioner, Rev. Tom Jewett, told those of us who had been coming for more than five years not to come the following year, so as to give other people a chance.

Freemasonry renounced

A couple of years after my release from yoga we went to a series of seminars at Bedford. One day when Mary was talking to Ione Carver, the subject of Freemasonry cropped up. I was summoned and explained to Ione that I had renounced and repented of my involvement. She explained that wives were also involved and under spiritual bondage. Would I repent again and this time include Mary? Too true I would! Kneeling down straight away between the two or them I did just that. From that moment Mary and I could pray together for the first time in our married life. Immediately afterwards we went to our room to make sure.

It is glorious news to be delivered from Satan's power, but how did I get into it in the first place? I knew that there was a need for salvation only available by the shed blood of Jesus, but ... let's go back to the beginning.

I was christened as a baby a few months old. My father was in the Royal Navy during the 1914–18 war and was sweeping mines in the Mediterranean at this time. When he returned home I was nearly four. To our mutual sorrow we had difficulty relating to each other. He was a great man and I missed out on much of the joy he desired to bestow upon me. He was a Free Churchman, my mother an Anglican, so as a consequence I was rarely taken to any place of worship.

When I was 16, however, my godparents suggested I

should be confirmed. If it made everybody else happy I was agreeable and duly went along to a couple of confirmation classes. I wasn't quite sure who was confirming what, but I certainly desired to know Jesus better. I meant business when the Bishop of Stafford laid his hands on my head and recited the set prayer in the 1662 Book of Common Prayer. Nobody had told me quite what to expect when I opened my eyes after he had finished. Would I see the Father? or Jesus? a score of angels perhaps? As I opened my eyes I would have settled for a couple of angels, but I saw no change whatsoever, nor did I feel different in any way. I felt disillusioned, let down. This was exacerbated when one of my sponsors asked me if I felt different. I didn't and I said so!

I did know a few Scriptures like John 14:12:

"Most assuredly, I say to you, he who believes in Me, the works that I do he will do also; and greater works than these he will do, because I go to My Father."

But I saw little reference to them in the round of worship I found in the Church of England. Jesus spoke the truth and here He prefaced a very sweeping statement with "Most assuredly", so this **must** be true!

Though I would not have put it that way then, whenever a miracle was encountered in the appointed lesson it was either ignored, explained or spiritualised. The son wasn't demon possessed, he had epilepsy or schizophrenia. Jesus just went along with the popular ideas of His day. What does it matter what an affliction is called as long as one is delivered from it? Bartimaeus didn't receive physical sight, just spiritual insight into the love

of God. Why then did he throw his yellow cloak away –
the symbol of his blindness corresponding to our white
stick?

I continued to attend church fairly regularly until I
joined the RAF. Here I attended church parades even
when not compulsory.

Into the occult

Towards the end of the 1939–45 war I met an instructor
who was a spiritualist. At the time I didn't know what
that meant. After a while I got myself invited to a
demonstration of psychometry and unwittingly started
on the path deeper into the occult. At first the "mes-
sages" were vague in the extreme, but that only
increased my determination to proceed further. Certainly there were quite a number of happenings which
could not be explained by the normal five senses.
Stupidly I equated the paranormal with Truth with a
capital "T".

I was not at peace in spiritism, so upon my release
from the Forces I consulted my rector. He admitted
that he knew very little about it but advised me to go to
the diocesan expert. I explained to this canon what I
had been getting up to and that I wasn't particularly
happy where I was going. His response was that I was
doing very well indeed and that I should keep at it! This
did little to quieten my unease at seances, but I kept
attending, though praying our Lord's prayer before
going.

After marrying Mary soon after the war I realised
that things weren't as happy and rosy as I would have
liked. One of my godparents, who had been reasonably
joyful, had been a Freemason, so I thought I would have
a go at that. Ten years or more later my affairs were

pretty appalling. On the face of things all was well, but happiness was a very rare visitor. Soon Mary mentioned divorce but I could not understand her point of view at all. The more I tried to convey my love and affection, the worse matters became.

Not tonight!

Whether I was seeking the Lord in spiritualism or the secrets of a Master Freemason, Jesus never seemed any closer or more real. Then when cycling to a seance as usual one Wednesday evening, I heard the Lord call out, "Not tonight!" His voice seemed loud enough to have been recorded if tape recorders had been invented. Praise the Lord, I responded to His call. I then learned from a special pal, a parson, where I was at, what I had been doing, and more significantly still where I was going – hell! When I remonstrated and asked why he had not told me all this before, he asked, "Would you have listened?"

There he had me. I do not think I would have done. Subsequently I discovered what had lain ahead of me that evening. If I had not been obedient to what I knew was of the Lord Jesus – I cannot explain why I knew – I should now be well on my way to hell, and that is not funny. The committee had decided to challenge me. Either I had to join them and accept their creed, or I was out! And I had been advised to continue in spiritualism by a canon of the Church of England!

As seen from the outside their creed is crazy. They agree that Jesus was a great man, a great prophet, probably the best medium there has ever been. But they disagree with most of what the Bible reports Him to have said. Jesus considered the risk of my agreeing to join them was too great, so He commanded me, "Not tonight!" What a tremendous Saviour I have!

There may have been a little lifting of the clouds over me then, but it did not help my relations with Mary and the boys. So it was in this parlous situation of imminent divorce that I first met John and Elsa Linden-Cook.

Fifteen years later the Lord spoke to both of us independently – to Mary while she was in hospital and to me during lunch at home. He told us the same thing – to be baptised in water, the believer's baptism. Thinking this was not exactly the best topic of conversation for a patient, I decided I would not mention it when I visited her that afternoon. But I opened my mouth to greet her and out it came. Mary then surprised me by responding that she had been discussing that very thing over lunch with the lady in the next bed but one. We resolved to obey as soon as Mary was sufficiently recovered.

I received yet another example of God's provision, as I drove back home one morning from the hospital after seeing Mary. The Lord drove the car off the straight main road, down a couple of side turnings. Then I could carry on driving. I cannot explain how He did this. A few moments later I saw a large chapel notice board which had painted across the bottom texts from Proverbs 3:5, 6:

> *"Trust in the Lord with all your heart, and lean not on your own understanding; in all your ways acknowledge Him, and He shall direct* (make straight or make plain) *your paths."*

A few days later when Mary was coming out of hospital I took her, and her sister who was staying with us, round that way to show them. The notice board had been taken away. God's timing is impeccable.

Jesus is faithful

While writing a book recently I realised that whatever divine authority has been bestowed upon me by John's ministry, this was not a spiritual re-birth. I reasoned that unless I had been a spiritual person, a child of my heavenly Father, then I could in no way have received a divine blessing. I knew I had received because of the works performed by the Father in the name of Jesus in my presence. So when was I born again? The Holy Spirit can bring all things to remembrance, so I asked Him. He showed me when and where very vividly, almost as if it had happened the day before. It was when I was around six years of age that I had asked Jesus into my life. Though I meant it at the time with all the sincerity of a youngster, I had wandered far away in my search for the evidence of the truth of John 14:12 and similar texts. All that time Jesus was faithful! In retrospect I can see the hand of the Lord in so many events that had seemed inexplicable at the time.

So, born again at six, confirmed at 16, when I should and may have received the fullness of the Holy Spirit, delivered and refilled with the Holy Spirit at 50 – is this the whole story? The answer must be an emphatic "No!" Rather it is just the beginning of the realisation of eternal life. Over the 20 years since that day of deliverance the Bible has become more and more exciting, so that former attractions, like science fiction, pale into complete insignificance.

Jesus said that He was sending His disciples into the world as the Father had sent Him (John 17:18). This is my experience. In His name I have healed the sick, cast out evil spirits and seen one dead man restored to life. I did not know he was dead when I prayed for him on the Euston to Glasgow train. Mary was an SRN when we married and had wide experience in Queen Alexandra's Nursing Service during the war. I am very glad for that man's sake and for my faith, that she did not tell me all the facts until after we had had dinner together that night. So changed was he that I did not recognise him as the same person in the hotel dining room.

Even all this is not anything to be really excited about, said Jesus. Have you ever read Luke 10:20? When His disciples returned to Jesus they were cock-a-hoop that the evil spirits were subject to them in His name. Jesus' reply puts the whole matter into its proper perspective:

> *"Nevertheless do not rejoice in this, that the spirits are subject to you, but rather rejoice because your names are written in heaven."*

That is really something – to know that for all eternity one is in the immediate company of Jesus and through Him, the Father. The Bible tells us that there is joy in heaven over one sinner that repents. Believe me, it is also a joy and privilege to witness it happen here on earth!'

Chapter 9

The Haunted Barn

David and Mary had moved from their bungalow in Ipswich and were now living in an old 15th century farmhouse a few miles away. We had been invited to speak at a meeting in the farmhouse that Saturday evening. David had sent us full directions and asked us to arrive in time for lunch around midday. The weather was good and we had little difficulty in finding the turn-off from the main road which would lead us to the farmhouse set in some five acres. The side road was little more than a cart track and we wondered what would happen if we met an oncoming vehicle – or a horse and cart! However, we had no such problems and were delighted at the scene as we turned into the drive. In front of us stood the farmhouse, not particularly large, but solid. The main stonework was painted white with black beams across the front. Beside the drive was quite a large pond, covered in duckweed. To one side of the farmhouse was a barn, about a third the size of the house and attached to it but, as we discovered later, with no connecting door. On our right were some other buildings. A typical small English farmstead. As we stopped the car, David and Mary came out to welcome us and we unloaded our things and went indoors.

David later related a story about the barn. His son was a talented pianist who also liked restoring old grand pianos, for which he used the adjoining barn. He was a sensible young man, not too long out of university, with his feet firmly on the ground. Yet one day, while working in the barn, he had felt a presence, though he knew no one else was there. He had looked round and seen a dark figure, which had disappeared when challenged. This experience had quite upset him and he insisted that he had not been dreaming. It soon became evident that what he had said was true. David had a large chow named Jane and had taken the dog into the barn shortly after his son's experience. The dog had walked in, then left quite hurriedly and thereafter refused to go into the barn. Having finished the story while we drank a welcome cup of tea, David then invited us to have a look in the barn.

A dog's discernment

The four of us went outside and into the barn, but Jane refused to come in with us. It was cool in the barn, cooler than one would have expected, and this seemed to be concentrated near the centre of the floor. The barn was partly furnished with a small table, a couple of chairs, a carpet and electric lighting. Personal items were dotted around the floor and the air was clean, not musty. It felt uncomfortable, yet there was no apparent reason for this – not surprising, for the cause was spiritual, not physical.

We suggested to David and Mary that we should take Communion in the barn and they readily agreed. We asked for a small glass of water to be brought in with the Communion things. We then prayed and asked for the guidance of the Holy Spirit. We prayed over the bread and the wine and each partook of these emblems of our Lord's death. After this we prayed over the glass of water, recognising that there was no power in the water itself, but that it was just a symbol of cleansing. Taking the water, we then proceeded round the barn, sprinkling the water over the floor and on the walls as we went with David in close attendance. The others joined with us as we commanded every unclean spirit to be subject to us. Then, standing near the middle of the barn, I commanded every unclean spirit to leave in the Name of Jesus. The dog, Jane, was sitting just outside the barn door, exactly where we had left her when we went in. Suddenly, as we commanded the evil spirit to depart, she gave one tremendous howl.

We sensed that something definite had taken place and David went to the door of the barn and opened it. Jane was standing just outside and David invited her, "Come on, then." Jane walked slowly into the barn and walked right round the walls, sniffing all the while. Arriving back at the door she went to the middle of the barn and sat down with her tail wagging! The place was clean. Never again was an apparition seen in the Walnut Tree Farm barn. The power of the name of Jesus had triumphed once again. Animals have a greater awareness of the spiritual world than we have and Jane knew when the evil spirit left the barn. Hence the howl and later her willingness to go into the barn and take possession of it.

Chapter 10

The Black Panther and the Chinese Dragon

'I was introduced to John and Elsa Linden-Cook whilst staying at the Christian Clinic for Environmental Medicine for treatment in 1990 by Pearl Coleman from whom I had received ministry when I first met her in Penang in 1988 and also in England later. During my stay of some 16 months at the Clinic, many members of her team discerned that I had a resident black panther spirit, which I found hard to accept. However, when an entirely independent born-again Christian visitor to the Clinic announced totally out of the blue that she had seen a black panther in the spirit with flaming yellow eyes in the clinic during my absence, I had to think again.

I had to admit that there were a few pointers to observe. I understood that my father kept a black panther when I was a small child and the government made him have it put down eventually. Also I always admired the big cat family for their stealth and special beauty. In Pakistan during the 12 years of my former heroin addiction I used to be fascinated by a film entitled *The Cat People*, where someone changed into a cat on the screen. Also I used to read a comic avidly as a small boy about a negro doctor who became a black panther at night and leapt from building to building with a radar device in his head, returning in the daytime to become a man. I used to say often, "Oh, I would like to be like that. I wish I could be a black panther..."

It is only now that I realise that because of what I was involved in as an addict – drugs, drug peddling, martial arts and violence – the devil didn't need a second invitation. People used to say I padded about and nobody would hear me coming. I believe this was true. Mind you, being an addict makes one stealthy! Knowing that John Linden-Cook was a man highly trusted and esteemed in Jesus by Pearl, I agreed to see him and Elsa. After a lengthy counselling they agreed to minister to me. I came home free of this awful demon and over a year later John told Pearl: "It was quite horrific that one. Have you heard of a werewolf, Pearl?" She replied "Yes." John continued, "Well there is obviously a spirit of a were-panther then – glaring eyes, claws, fangs, roaring. It's a good job one knows one's authority at such times!"

A life-changing ministry

A second time I was ministered to by John and Elsa whom I had come to trust, though I was extremely humiliated having twice backslidden on heroin after knowing such wonderful freedom due to the ministry of Pearl. Through John and Elsa I received an incredible life-changing ministry. At the time I was harbouring a lot of pride and rejection and it wasn't easy for me, but Pearl knew the axe had to be laid to the root of the tree. John and Elsa's discernment was incredible, and all the things that had been discerned in the spirit at Pearl's turned out to be true. But something amazing happened. During ministry a spirit named itself "Akhtar". It came out with blood, as did all the martial arts spirits which followed. Also there was a spirit of bitterness towards God. John and Elsa had no idea that when I went to Pakistan at the age of 17 I was met and controlled by a man called "Akhtar". He was a violent man who introduced me to the life of heroin, martial arts, violence and drug-pushing. I went to Pakistan totally innocent and I was taken over by this man who controlled both the judiciary and police in the area where we stayed, as well as a good proportion of the population. In fact I became "proud" of being close to him.

Also as a small child, from birth until about the age of six, I was brought up by Chinese nurses and an Indian nurse. They washed and dressed and fed me as my Mum was ill when I was born. I did recall being taken to the temple and things being done to me but I didn't recall exactly what. Elsa told me that from the moment of conception I had had to fight for life. This was true as my Mum did not want an eighth child and considered abortion. Also at birth a pronouncement was made over me as I was born jaundiced, that I could live or die. Praise God, I lived! Elsa discerned that I had been horribly beaten as a baby and small child, which had driven a real anger into me through total helplessness. I just knew that what she was discerning was from God – and so the deliverance proved. A Chinese dragon spirit, which had been discerned through a vision given to one of Pearl's team at the Clinic some time before, came out with blood and also spirits of insane violence, anger and schizophrenia. When I was anointed on my hands and feet with oil I felt it burn red hot – it was like fire. When Elsa put the oil on my forehead it felt also like I was being clawed. I kept checking my head to see if it was blood.

I am deeply grateful to the Lord Jesus for His ministers, John and Elsa, and I know that what the Lord has begun in me He will bring to completion. Hallelujah! I give God all the glory. How many people are there, I wonder, like me under total self-condemnation but with nowhere to go? I thank God for both John and Elsa's ministry as well as that of Pearl.'

Chapter 11

Head or Heart Salvation?

In Chapter 3 of the Gospel of John we read of a man named Nicodemus, a ruler of the Jews and a Pharisee, who came to Jesus by night. During that secret meeting with the Saviour, the Lord Jesus confronted Nicodemus with an amazing statement: unless Nicodemus was born again he could not see the Kingdom of God! Nicodemus' response was quite natural for a man looking at the statement from a purely physical standpoint. How could a man possibly enter his mother's womb and be born yet again? It was impossible, yet that seemed to be what the Lord Jesus was saying. Jesus then went on to explain. When we are born naturally we are 'born of water' – a baby in its mother's womb is surrounded by water. We are all born of water, born of the flesh – but not yet born of the Spirit. The Lord Jesus is referring to the Holy Spirit, the Spirit of love, purity, holiness, the eternal Spirit. So being born again means a complete change for a human being, a translation from this worldly kingdom of darkness and the flesh into the Kingdom of the Lord Jesus, the Kingdom of Light and the Holy Spirit.

Today we live in a science-orientated world, the so-called technological age. 'Your mind is the master, not your conscience or your heart.' The mind makes people strive for more and more things because they yearn to go one better than the neighbours. Their hearts are subject to their minds, so they start to love the things of the world, become more and more egotistic, and in the end 'every man wants to do what seems right in his own eyes'. It has become a way of life, taught in schools, in special workshops for 'success' in your business, and is often accompanied by instructions in yoga, relaxation exercises, mind control and the teachings the New Age gurus have unloaded on an unsuspecting public.

Our heart's needs and our spiritual hunger for something deeper than these things that will pass away is ignored. It is not difficult to understand that many people who hear the message of salvation and eternal life hear it only with their minds, and as their hearts are subject to their minds the message does not touch their hearts.

Salvation or intellectual agreement?

Our minds are all too willing to agree with all kinds of propositions, often just to please another. Many folks have gone forward at a salvation call given at a meeting because they thought it was expected of them by the person who brought them. Or perhaps they thought it was expected of them so they could become one of the group. Others want to be left alone and hope that if they go forward at a meeting their family or friends will stop pestering them. Some may think, 'I will give it a trial. Perhaps it will be good for me.' So it happens that people accept the salvation the Lord Jesus offers with their minds alone. Their hearts are untouched. The prophet Jeremiah pointed out that the human heart is deceitful and beyond cure! If the heart is beyond cure, how can the mind change it? The mind can only deceive the heart, not change it.

Sometimes I wonder how many meetings I had been to before I realised that I only related to the Lord Jesus with my mind. I knew the Bible well and could easily pick on wrong teaching and argue about religious points. People probably thought I was a good Christian. After all, I had been to church for about 30 years, I was sure I had a passport to eternal life and the Lord Jesus would welcome me, for I had been a good church member all these years. But one can go to someone's house and not meet them. I have been into Buckingham Palace on business on several occasions and yet I did not meet the Queen. I would have to admit that I do not know her. I know **of** her and a lot **about** her, but I do not **know** her. A great many of those who go to church are like that. They know of God, they know about God, but they do not **know** God. There is no personal relationship, it is only in their minds. After listening to a preacher I realised in my innermost being that I longed for a close relationship with the Lord Jesus. But how could I obtain it? It sounds so easy – 'You must be born again' – but how does it happen and what do I have to do for it to happen?

We read how Peter told the people on the Day of Pentecost when the Holy Spirit came on to this earth, that they must repent. Paul, writing to the Christians in Rome, wrote,

> *'If you confess with your mouth the Lord Jesus and believe in your heart that God has raised Him from the dead, you will be saved* (delivered, healed). *For with the heart one believes to righteousness, and with the mouth confession is made to salvation.'*

A changed heart – Salvation!

We have to believe with the heart, not with the mind. I can say from experience that to believe with the heart means to renounce one's great ideas about one's self, one's family, one's achievements, and look at self with the eyes of the Lord Jesus. I compared myself, my way of life, my relationships and my attitudes, with those of the Lord Jesus and was very ashamed. Then I understood what Peter meant when he said to Jesus after the miraculous catch of fish, *'Depart from me, for I am a sinful man, O Lord!'*

Only with my heart can I truly repent of my sins and iniquity. My mind will always find intellectual excuses for my wrong deeds, thoughts and words. So often 'it was the other person's fault!' Close to our heart is our conscience which seems to me to be a kind of recorder. Everything we have ever done, thought or said, good or bad, seems to be stored in that memory. Though it is like a tape recorder, you cannot erase any of it! The Holy Spirit is the Master Who plays these 'tapes' back to us! Though we cannot erase them, they can be 'overplayed' with the blood of Jesus. This has the effect, as far as God is concerned, of erasing not only the memories but the sin represented by them and giving us a clean tape.

But Satan knows our past evil acts and uses the information to accuse us. Sometimes people are tormented by their sins, not realising that there is a way out. There is forgiveness and cleansing through the shed blood of Jesus. We are told in Hebrews 9:22 that there is no forgiveness of sins without shedding of blood, and in Leviticus 17:11 we read that it is the blood that makes atonement for the soul. That was why the Lord commanded Israel to sacrifice perfect animals, so that their blood, the life of the creature, was given in exchange for the condemned human life. God, not man, ordained this way of forgiveness for His ancient people. It is interesting that the Jews were the only people who embodied forgiveness in their religion. That privilege has now been transferred to those who are born again – that is, Christians. Ours is the only religion on earth which offers reconciliation with God. In all other religions there is no forgiveness. When God was about to judge Egypt on the night of the first Passover, when the angel of death would kill all the first-born of the land of Egypt, man or beast, He told the Children of Israel through Moses that they must put the blood on the doorposts and lintels of their dwellings.

> *'When I see the blood, I will pass over you; and the plague shall not be on you to destroy you when I strike the land of Egypt.'*

This was a foreshadowing of the Lord Jesus becoming a sacrifice for us when He went to the Cross of Calvary. His blood was shed to redeem us from death and eternal condemnation. If we accept this and confess our need of a Saviour, then our sins are forgiven. When the Lord God sees us washed in the blood of the Lord Jesus, He will not see our evil human nature, but a new creature in the Lord Jesus. The word the Lord Jesus spoke to Nicodemus that night will then have become a reality in our life – we will have been born again. As the Apostle Paul wrote,

> *'If anyone is in Christ, he is a new creation; old things have passed away; behold, all things have become new.'*   (2 Corinthians 5:17)

Mind salvation only changes one pattern of living for

106

another by a conscious effort of the will. Such people have to remember not to swear any more; they think they have to give up going down to the pub with the boys, give up smoking and other things, and they struggle to give them up, mostly without success. The person who is born again finds that these things give **them** up. They no longer have a desire for them. There has been such a wonderful change in their personality, they believe with their heart and know the real meaning of forgiveness. Those with head salvation do not know the meaning of real forgiveness or experience it. How can they? From talking with people I find many are like that. They have no peace in their heart. There is no assurance of salvation. Jesus is no more real to them now than He was before. But when forgiveness is real they are born again of the heart. They know the peace the Lord Jesus said would be ours and which He would leave with us.

Our memory – a supernatural tape recorder

I mentioned before that our conscience seems to have a memory like the tape of a tape recorder. All our misdeeds are there and Satan, our accuser, often uses our memories of past sins to condemn us. But once we have accepted that the blood of the Lord Jesus has washed our sins away and that the Lord God will not remember them any more, as He has promised, provided we repent, Satan will not be able to torment us. We know in our hearts that we have been accepted by our heavenly Father and that there is now no condemnation. We can then boldly say to Satan when he reminds us of some past sin, 'Satan, I distinctly remember forgetting that, just as God has.'

One winter many years ago I threw a snowball and

broke our neighbour's window. Later my father tackled me about it and I admitted that I had done it, and said I was sorry. I was not only sorry, but I was very frightened at what might now happen to me. But my father said, 'All right, I will see to it.' The window was repaired and the incident never mentioned again. My father had forgiven me and I knew he would not say in six months time, 'You broke that window in the winter and now I am going to give you a hiding for it.' No, I was forgiven. That was the end of the matter. So it is with God. When we realise His total forgiveness in our spirit we have peace but that can only be yours if your heart has been born again.

For believers only

I have come to realise from counselling many people that a great many church-goers are not born again. But this is the starting point if a person needs deliverance from evil spirits. Deliverance ministry is for believers, not unbelievers. If a demon is cast out of an unbeliever, it will probably soon be occupying its old home again, for it is empty. It may well bring seven others with it, worse than itself! The Holy Spirit has not been allowed to move in and, as the Lord Jesus said, the last state of that person is worse than the first.

I find this is also true of people with head salvation. The mind cannot be born again, so there is no room for the Holy Spirit to work. The evil spirits may leave when commanded to do so but they will soon be back. That may be why we so often hear of people who have had deliverance ministry and seem to have the same problems and manifestations again. To be born again is a work of the Holy Spirit – don't think it can be achieved by just counselling. Thousands in our churches have been baptised and many of them confirmed, yet they exhibit none of the marks or signs of being born again.

What are the marks and signs?

These marks or signs are clearly set out in the Bible, the word God has given us by which we can judge and evaluate all things. The first is found in the First Letter of John. In 1 John 3:9 we read,

> *'Whoever has been born of God does not sin, for His seed remains in him; and he cannot sin, because he has been born of God.'*

Then again in 1 John 5:18 we find that,

> *'We know that whoever is born of God does not sin; but he who has been born of God keeps himself, and the wicked one does not touch him.*

A person who is born again does not continue to sin as a habit. This is not to say he will never sin, but, as 1 John 1:8, 9 states,

> *'If we say that we have no sin, we deceive ourselves, and the truth is not in us. If we confess our sins, He is faithful and just to forgive us our sins and to cleanse us from all unrighteousness.'*

A person who is truly born again does not deliberately continue in a sinful way of life. He no longer sins with his heart (his mind, will and emotions) like someone who is not born again. But the heart is deceitful and desperately wicked, so the only remedy is crucifixion of self and a new birth. In other words, sin is no longer a pleasure, but abhorrent to him. He hates the very thought of it. As Paul tells us in Romans 7:23, he sees a law at work in himself at war with his mind, a war which brings him into captivity to the law of sin in him. The only One who can deliver him from this body of death is Jesus Christ, through whom he could be born again. Paul does not say that he has no sin, but rather that there is a way out. His great longing and desire is not to commit sin any more. Well might Paul say in Romans 12:2 that we should not be conformed to this world, but be transformed by the renewing of our minds.

We can also know a person is born again by 1 John 5:1:

> 'Whoever believes that Jesus is the Christ is born of God.'

When we are born again of the Spirit of God we fully believe that Jesus Christ is the only Saviour and that there is no other way to the Father in heaven – and that only because of that precious blood shed for the atonement of our sin. One realises that Jesus Christ is the One appointed by God alone and there is no other. Christ Jesus came into the world for this very purpose, to destroy the works of the devil. Apart from Jesus there is no hope, no forgiveness, no peace, no reconciliation with God – only a fearful expectation of hell fire!

We see nothing in ourselves which would warrant our going to heaven. We know that, compared to Him, any righteousness we thought we had is as filthy rags in his sight. But through Jesus we consider ourselves dead to sin and alive to God. We have total confidence that through His shed blood all our sins are forgiven and we are made righteous in God's sight because of the finished work of Jesus accomplished on the Cross of

Calvary. Such a person knows full well that his hope of eternal life does not rest on his good works, his achievements, his giving, his prayers, nor even the church he belongs to, but solely on the finished work of Jesus.

The third distinguishing mark or sign of a truly born again Christian is in 1 John 2:29:

> *'You know that everyone who practises righteousness is born of Him.'*

Someone who is born again seeks to live according to the will of God, to do what is pleasing to God, to carry out the Great Commission in whatever area of service he is called to. Such a person has a desire and longing in his heart to love the Lord his God with all his heart, with all his soul and with all his mind, and his neighbour as himself. He will always look to the Lord Jesus Christ as his example, or role-model (and who better?), and seek to be obedient to all Christ's commands. He is not perfect, as he would be the first to admit, but fights the urge to sin which assails him from time to time. He knows the reality of the war Paul spoke of in Romans 7, which tries to draw him away from doing God's will. Yet, whatever his shortcomings, his desire and longing remain steadfast. By the grace of God he seeks to be holy, for that is the command. He may even question from time to time whether he is a true Christian, but he would no doubt agree with John Newton's words,

> 'I am not what I ought to be, I am not what I want to be, I am not what I hope to be in another world; but still I am not what I once used to be, and by the grace of God, I am what I am.'

Some people believe that belonging to a particular

church and taking part in its rites and ceremonies – infant baptism and confirmation; baptism by immersion; or attending Mass and doing penance; or any other ritual – makes them a Christian and a born-again believer. But in truth none of these will get us to heaven. Only those who exhibit the signs and marks I have mentioned are truly born again. Those who do not show these signs and marks in their lives are not born again. Do you have these signs? Are you born again? In the next chapter you can read the story of one who thought she was born again but realised one day that she had only head salvation, not heart salvation.

Chapter 12

I Finally Found Heart Salvation

'As the train chugged along beside the rocky river on a damp summer afternoon during World War II the low mountains seemed to close in on me ominously. In retrospect, I think I must have sensed the spiritual darkness of the area. Our family soon settled into lodgings with a kind landlady. Her husband was kind too and a regular chapel-goer, but he had to be persuaded to let us **use** the bath, not just keep it as a status symbol!

Being shy, I did not try to make friends with the village youngsters, but went for walks, sometimes with my parents but often alone. The river, lakes and mountains soon had me by the heartstrings. I delighted in sitting on a rock in the middle of the river and being mesmerised by the sound and look of the water as it gurgled and rushed over the stones and splashed over boulders. My feet and hands had to be in the water however cold it was.

I often wandered through the pine forests to the top of the nearest mountain from whose flattish rough rocky top I could look right down on to the village. Alone there, I felt queen of all I surveyed. I danced barefoot as I gazed at the other higher mountains in the distance

and the setting sun. The exhilaration and sense of freedom had to be experienced to be understood. I felt I was
only truly alive at such times.

What deception! Idolatry of mountains – one mountain in particular – was starting to bind me. The mild
rainy days were my joy as I stood by the river and felt
the soft rain on my face and hair, then wandered to a
part of the riverside walk where I could look at my
favourite mountain, provided it was not shrouded in
mist. Though it was seven miles away I often spoke to it
by name. I was worshipping the creation rather than the
Creator.

Rowena played the organ in the Church of Wales
which I attended in the village. I had rarely gone to
church before that. We became friendly and I often
went for walks with her after the service, talking at
great length. I was a teenager, but she was an adult. She
took me to a spiritist's house to see the stuffed animals –
horrid freaks! I was not aware at the time that the lady
was a spiritist, but I picked up the house's oppressive
atmosphere. Rowena was very fond of her country. We
were friends in Wales for about three years, then I
returned to London. But by then a telepathic friendship
had developed and we often knew what the other was
doing or thinking – as our letters confirmed.

The pull of Wales

Wales and the Welsh were mine by heart adoption,
especially the village, the church and the surrounding
streams, rivers, lakes and mountains. I often said that
the natural scenery of North Wales meant more to me
than any person could and that I could never love anyone more than I loved North Wales. You get what you
say, so it was like putting a curse on myself. When I later

joined the Norwood Christian Fellowship I could not bear anyone to hug me in a Christian embrace. I would not and could not accept love. I had to confess, renounce and repent of my words about loving scenery more than people, then I gradually became able to accept love and love others too.

From 1948 to 1964 I returned to the village each year for a holiday. Each time I felt a greater heartache at leaving, though Rowena was now living in England. The mountains and rivers held me. Welsh hymns sung in Welsh stirred my emotions more than anything else except for the Welsh anthem *Land of My Fathers*. Yet my ancestry is English with a little Scots blood.

In 1965 I went to a Christian holiday conference in Aberystwyth. This meant little to me, apart from a trip to the National Eisteddfod at Newtown. It was all in Welsh, but we were given "translator sticks" to provide an English commentary. That day's special ceremony was the Chairing of the Bard. The scene was colourful. The Druids were dressed in turquoise and green and were entertained by young maidens dancing, bearing sheaves of corn and the fruits of the earth to offer them. The Druids held strange yet attractive wands made of a transparent Perspex-like material with gold symbols on them. We got the impression that the dances were connected with fertility rites. The highlight for me was rising to sing *Land of My Fathers* in Welsh with all the Welsh people and feeling at one with them.

Looking back at that scene now, it seems grotesque – those men in weird head-dresses and robes carrying wands – utterly non-Christian – reverencing the Bard because he wrote the best poetry. *Pears Encyclopedia* states that Druidism and Christianity are unrelated and that the Druid priests were finally wiped out about

AD 58 on the Isle of Anglesey, their last stronghold. Christianity can certainly have no links with the Druids.

Some time between 1965 and 1972 Rowena remarried and wrote to tell me she would no longer use that name, as her new husband did not wish her to have a Welsh name. I think, judging by his surname, that he was part Jewish. To drop her Welsh name seemed sacrilege to me, so I wrote to tell her I would not write to her again. After all, she had played a key part in helping me to love Wales and the Welsh.

I was confirmed in the Church of Wales in 1944 and after that was a regular weekly communicant in the Church of England, though it meant little to me. The Lord led me from the church I attended to the one where John and Elsa worshipped. I joined their Bible Study group too after their vicar suggested it would be good to do so. John and Elsa later invited me to visit them one evening for deliverance ministry.

That very day I received a letter from Rowena, though I had not heard from her for many years, begging me to contact her again. The spiritual pull to do so was still very strong, but by then I trusted John and Elsa and knew that something was preventing me from loving Jesus Christ as they did. So I agreed to destroy the letter from Rowena. That was the start of the battle to let Jesus free me from the spiritism that had its claws in me through Rowena. I later confessed, renounced and repented of the soul-tie between me and Rowena in the name of Jesus and had it severed with the sword of the Holy Spirit. The friendship was not morally wrong, as it led me to love good music and to be kinder to other people. Rowena was very kind to everyone but she had many spiritist friends, as I learned last year from some-one who used to live near her, and so she obviously did not truly love the Lord God and I was certainly tainted.

While I lived in Wales I bought a pair of dark blue hair slides from a local shop and often wore them. But I could remember feeling the pressure of them on my head when seated in Fairy Glen with Rowena. They were thrown away long ago but the occult power associated with them had to be broken. Fairy Glen was dark and gloomy too – not a nice place to sit. So John and Elsa broke the occult powers in the name of Jesus Christ and His blood cleansed me.

I was obsessed with Wales and the Welsh people and especially the village where we stayed during the war, so if I was ever within 50 miles I just had to get there and sit on the rocks in the rivers and get on the mountain tops. I was **frantic** till I did. When I was in a group of Spirit-filled people worshipping the Lord, I was like two people. Outwardly I wanted to join in the worship, but inside I was feeling like snarling and my mouth wanted to grin. This part of me wanted to be free to return to Wales, free to dance on the mountain tops and wallow in the streams. So I asked John and Elsa for a further deliverance appointment. During that evening I suddenly saw an ugly little red dragon on my mind – not like the one on the Welsh flag, but unmistakably a demon linked to Wales. So at John's suggestion I told it that I had confessed, renounced and repented of my idolatry of Wales and everything Welsh, so it had no ground to claim in my life. It was to go in Jesus' name. After a while, it did with some coughing and I knew that I was free of my Welsh obsession after more than 40 years. I no longer thrill to hear the Welsh accent. Last year while staying in mainly English-speaking Montgomery in Powys, my friend asked if I'd like her to take me to the village that I knew so well. I was able to say, "No, thank you," quite easily and with no regrets. Praise the Lord!

Still there was the pull of the sea – "I must get my feet in the waves." The Holy Spirit revealed to John and Elsa that it could be a nymph spirit, so they ministered along those lines after I had confessed, renounced and repented of the hold that the sea had on me. There was quite a reaction! I later stayed in Eastbourne for a few days but had no urge to paddle, which was unheard of previously. Glory to Jesus!

During each deliverance session, I was told to breathe in the Holy Spirit after evil spirits had been cast out, to fill the gap where they had been ousted in Jesus' name.

My parents were very respectable people and their parents and families were well respected in the small towns they lived in. Yet from somewhere I had inherited some occultism. I was also fascinated with books about witchcraft and Satan. One of my aunts no doubt helped in this, as she would make up adventures and help me to join in the stories as a child. The witch always loomed large, even when she wrote to me when I was a teenager.

Soul-ties broken

Once an adult, but before knowing Jesus Christ as Lord, I had formed wrong relationships with some men friends, but after meeting John and Elsa, part of me longed to know and love Jesus as they so obviously did, but I could not. One by one, as I was willing, I confessed, renounced and repented of the wrong friendships of the past, had the soul-ties cut and, of course, had to throw out any gifts that would link me to those memories. One gift was a pair of antique mirrors – very pretty and seemingly harmless. It took all my will power to take them from the hooks on the wall and dispose of them. I trembled all over as I did so. It was not the sentimental attachment, but something to do with the mirrors themselves. Perhaps what they had "seen" as they hung on the landing in another house? Anyway, there was peace once they were in the rubbish bin. It is unwise to have second-hand furniture or clothes, unless one knows all about the previous owner. Some objects which I needed to throw away were well known to my relatives so they would be likely to notice if they went missing. I worried about this, especially if they were valuable, because my family was very money-conscious. But I realised that the God who set me free could stop people noticing that things had disappeared. So I asked the Holy Spirit to blind their eyes to the missing objects. He answered wonderfully every time.

Rebellion is as witchcraft or the sin of divination as it says in 1 Samuel 15:23. I can well remember being at a Christian Holiday Conference in 1967, when the leader told us we could, then should clap as we sang, "I was lost but Jesus found me." My arms were firmly folded and I would not clap, though they sang that chorus many times. Rebellion! Years later, while casting out a demon, my friends said to it, "You **will** kneel at the foot of the Cross!" In my body it had to, in the name of Jesus. So much rebellion and witchcraft had gone over the years, otherwise I would have refused to bow down.

Until last year I preferred dimly lit church services and Bible studies and dimly lit prayer meetings. Something in me felt exposed in full light. Many a time when the Holy Spirit has been present in power in a meeting, I have felt explosive. Sometimes I have gone home without saying "Good night!" to my friends, so strongly did the evil in me react to the power of the Holy Spirit. Praise God, He always drew me back to the next meeting, even after I had run out. I knew that if I wanted to

119

be able to love Jesus, I had to stay where the Presiding Elder knew his Bible and believed it 100%.

I **did** want to love Jesus Christ like other members of the Fellowship. I saw the difference in their eyes. When talking with them I knew that they loved Jesus and wanted to live Christ-centred lives. As mentioned, I was confirmed in the Church of Wales and was a Sunday School teacher. I was on the Parochial Church Council in the Church of England and organised Bible Study weekends, yet I still sometimes blatantly and deliberately sinned, because my heart did not belong to Jesus.

At the end of a Christian holiday house party in 1961, an appeal was made for everyone who did not really know Jesus to let Him into every area of their mind. Or were there some rooms in our mind that we did not want Him to see? So I said "Sorry!" to Jesus and asked Him to guide me in everything and come into every room in my mind. As I returned home to an empty house, I had no fear as before, for Jesus was with me. But then the battle began. I wanted to live life my way, pleasing my friends and myself. As Jesus had a hold on only some of my mind, I naturally lived for human relationships, many of them wrong and for the sheer exhilaration of the countryside. Despite this, the Lord graciously gave me a touch of His power on Whit Sunday, May 29, 1966. Soon after I was shown a vision that I knew was for me. The interpretation was, "Ignore the Blood at your peril," so I dutifully continued taking Holy Communion, though it meant nothing to me.

I first met John and Elsa in 1972 and was soon in Bible studies with the Norwood Christian Fellowship. Then I received some deliverance ministry which began to change me. I had been an avid reader, particularly of romantic novels, for most of my life. These are pure fantasy and led me into more imagining with myself as the heroine. This let in many an evil spirit, so, once I was willing much renewing of my mind was necessary (Romans 12:2). A degree of peace came, but I was still aware that I resented having to live as Jesus taught and not as I wanted. There was no love for Jesus in my heart, though my mind told me that I should be grateful that He had died in my place, taking my sins to the Cross and cutting Himself off from God, His Father. As 1 John 3 points out,

> *"Whoever is born of God does not habitually sin and if he does sin* (occasionally but not deliberately) *the precious blood of Jesus cleanses us."*

But I was still at times walking into sin knowingly.

The Outreach Meetings faced me with a new challenge. John kept talking about the Airlift or Rapture and that *"You must be born again"* (John 3). Was I born again? I asked myself. Elsa and Barbara said I was, but I felt I was not, though I raised my arms in praise, spoke in tongues and even danced in praise and worship at times. I knew I had given my mind to Jesus in the summer of 1961, but something still suddenly took me over at times. The Bible then became dull and Christianity boring. I usually gloated inwardly on the way home from Bible studies, prayer meetings or church, as I was now free to please myself until the next meeting. I knew this was not the right attitude for a Christian, even though pleasing myself did not involve anything evil. So I began to ask God to show me what was wrong. Why couldn't I love Him as John, Elsa and Barbara did? One Sunday in autumn 1992, during our time of worship at church, the Holy Spirit showed me a toy gas stove, doll's house size. As I looked at it, puzzled, I realised that I had owned one like it as a child, along with a kettle and three little saucepans. I shared this with my friend on the way home and she prayed aloud in the car that the Lord would reveal to me why He had showed it to me. I asked this too as I drove into the garage. As I switched off the engine, I heard in my mind, as clearly as if it had been audible, the words, "You're playing with Me." This shocked me and I asked, "How?" The answer was equally clear, reminding me of artificial praises when my heart was not right with Him.

Going to my own funeral!

One day when I was talking to Elsa on the phone, she asked if I had ever been to my own funeral. As she continued talking, almost praying, on the phone, I began to feel desperately sad, lonely and empty inside, and lost. I had never felt like it before. She talked about throwing away all my good deeds – which are no use, of course – out of a train window. I felt desolate that evening, but the Lord was obviously in her words.

A few days later I heard John's tape on *Head or Heart Salvation* and knew that I did not have heart salvation. I told John this and asked how I should get it. I could not go forward at an Outreach Meeting to be "born again" as I had been forward before, when Steve Ryder came, though nothing obvious happened then. John said, "See how the Spirit leads." So on 21st November, 1992, I hardly heard John's talk, as I was determined to get heart salvation that night.

When he asked those who wanted to be born again to go forward, I was inwardly praying, "Lord, show me how and when to get forward." I had an aching tightness in my left rib cage, though physically I was well. As John walked past me down the aisle he said, "Come forward if you have never come forward before," so I could not. I was trembling and in a panic but waited till the special needs were being met for those John had called forward after a word of knowledge. Then I queued and prayed. "Lord, please take me to the right person to pray for me." There was Elsa, just chatting, so I told her that I wanted real heart salvation and to be truly born again of the Holy Spirit. She led me in yet another prayer of confession, renunciation and repentance, and asking Jesus into my heart. The trembling in my left rib cage got worse as I thanked Jesus for loving me and coming into my heart as I gave it to Him.

Then I remembered that John had told me to ask the Holy Spirit to show me when to go forward for something else. Deliverance was necessary too. As I confessed, renounced and repented of a Jezebel spirit – a spirit of controlling others – the trembling gradually ceased and I knew that I had been freed by the power of Jesus' name. John then prayed for a new infilling of the Holy Spirit. I felt light and slightly wobbly as His power came into me, then I returned to my place. The rest of the meeting passed normally with others being set free and healed.

The next day, Sunday, I took the bread and wine at Communion and realised there was no longer any barrier to it. I could accept Jesus' blood as cleansing me from any sins which I had unthinkingly committed – such as impatience with people or driving faster than the law allows. I felt a new joy and peace.

That Sunday I asked the Lord to show me anything that I still needed to get rid of. He did. There were photos of the church in Wales that had spiritist memories, a dress I had once worn on a visit to a man friend, and a beautiful ring which I treasured. When I looked at the ring in its box, I realised the evil pull it had. There was a short battle, then I threw it away. All these tainted things have now gone, praise the Lord!

I love Jesus Christ. I know that I love Him and I know I'm born again and that I received heart salvation in November, 1992.

My thought patterns have changed since then. When I return home from Bible studies, prayer meetings or church services, I still want to read the Bible and feel just as free at the meetings as at home. I am the same person in all places, though I love being with other born-again believers. I am at peace in all our meetings, rejoicing in the Lord Jesus Christ and in my heavenly Father, and at the Holy Spirit working in other people's lives.

There have been slight temptations, but immediately I begin to experience one, I tell Satan that Jesus is my Lord and to **go** in His name. The Holy Spirit has brought Bible passages to my mind, such as 1 Corinthians 10:13, Psalm 91 or John 15. I thank Jesus for His love, which keeps me free and rejoicing, for I want to live as He wants.

Spirit or spirits?

Up to 21st November, 1992 I usually kept some alcohol in the larder, in case I felt low or depressed. I often drank a couple of glasses of Drambuie or three of gin and tonic late at night, or in the daytime even when I was not depressed. I drank alone, as no one else in our house drinks. I was not happy to be without alcohol in the house, though I have not drunk to excess of recent years – nor wanted to. After Christmas I suddenly realised there was an unopened bottle of Drambuie in the larder. It was no use to me now so I threw it away. My body is a temple of the Holy Spirit (1 Corinthians 6:19) so I need no other spirits!

Shortly after this I was truly born again. I was amazed to realise that my lifelong need for a husband – since the age of ten anyway – was no longer there. It had slipped away when I asked Jesus Christ into my heart. If the right man came along, I'd accept the chance of married life, but whereas I once thought when the Rapture was mentioned, "Not until I've had some married bliss!" my chief concern now is to be ready and looking for Jesus' return, no matter whether I miss out on a lazy retirement or a husband. So come quickly, Lord Jesus.

The bread and wine in the Lord's Supper symbolise what Jesus did for me. He bore my rotten sins on the Cross and was cut off from His Father for three hours, since God could not look at Jesus as He became sin on my behalf.

It is joyous to know that Jesus loves me, and I love Him because He loves me. It is so wonderful to know that I am born again and have heart salvation after all those years of dryness and uncertainty. Jesus Christ has set me free from so much evil that I invited into my life. His name is all powerful today. God the Father is so loving and forgiving because Jesus, His Son, offered His blood for you and me.

Jesus the Christ is the only way to God the Father. Jesus defeated Satan on the Cross. As a favourite hymn puts it:

"For this purpose Christ was revealed
To destroy all the works of the evil one.
Christ in us has overcome,
So with gladness we sing
And welcome his Kingdom in." '

✻   ✻   ✻

The name Rowena used in this testimony is not the real name of the lady concerned and has been used to protect her identity.

Chapter 13

Healed of ME

'Having spent my childhood in a Roman Catholic orphanage, I moved around a lot until my mid-twenties, working in a variety of jobs in this country and abroad. I am amazed how I ever survived some of the things that happened to me. But now I realise the good Lord was always with me, guiding and, wherever necessary gently tugging me back on to the road He had chosen for me.

As a boy, I didn't really want to know about God, mainly as a response to the teaching methods used in the orphanage. When I arrived there, aged six, the head priest tested my knowledge of the Bible and my response was so poor that he decided I should have extra religious instruction. We spent many tedious hours in the classroom and the church being bombarded with Bible quotations. We were expected to make notes on them, then later look them up in the Bible and learn them. I also had great difficulty reading, writing and spelling, as I am dyslexic. But I was then categorised as a lazy, stupid, good-for-nothing and put into a class of "slow learners" – that is, the most stupid.

Nothing was done to help me with my learning difficulties, but I **did** learn to fight. What could anyone expect in a class of nut cases? We were punished for this almost every day – six of the best with a cane or belt, or yet more texts to learn from the Bible. I chose corporal punishment as it was easier to take.

When I was 14 they arranged for me to move into a boarding house run by a religious Irishwoman. I was very excited when I first heard about this. We didn't have much contact with women, so for a time I became the envy of every boy in the class. But my ideas changed when I met this giant 6ft 2in Irishwoman. The look of horror on my face made the priest chuckle as he put my bag down outside the front door of the boarding house and I could still hear him laughing as he disappeared into the dark night. Then a deep rough Irish voice said behind me, "Are you going to be standing out there all night with your mouth wide open, or would you mind picking up your bag and coming in here before you have me letting out all of God's good warm air?"

"Yes, Ma'am," I said, hurriedly picking up my bag and edging past her into the hallway. She led me to a small bedroom at the back of the house and showed me the bathroom. Then she started to enumerate the rules of the house. I stared at her round, expressionless face, thinking that this place sounded worse than where I had come from. At the first opportunity I would get out.

My first job down at the docks had been arranged for me. It was hard work shovelling coal all day from the coal boats in Derry docks into one-ton buckets, so I kept my eyes open for other work. I never regretted taking a job with a travelling circus, but unfortunately this wonderful taste of freedom lasted only two years. When the circus returned to England it fell upon hard times and some of us, including me, had to leave.

I was by now a 16-year-old lapsed Roman Catholic trying to keep out of trouble, find more work and get on with living. My circus life taught me to be totally independent and look after number one. I enjoyed moving around, accountable to no one, so I took work on building sites or with road gangs – jobs which usually provided accommodation. It was pretty rough, but it suited most of the men. Weekends were usually pretty lively after Friday and Saturday nights drinking in the town. As I didn't drink, I tried to keep clear when the fighting broke out, but sometimes I got caught up in it, so I started to learn karate.

Martial arts

I was involved with the martial arts for over 25 years, visiting many dojos all over England and in Europe, learning and later teaching different styles of karate. As a Christian, I now know karate is occult. You have to remove your shoes before entering a dojo, because it is holy ground, and many dojos contain pictures, statues or even altars you must bow to on entering or leaving.

The main reason for learning karate is to injure or even kill one's opponent. It was developed by monks in China, who were not allowed to use weapons, but needed to defend themselves. The soldiers who attacked them were amazed at their skill, so when peace came the monks taught them their skills. The knowledge spread and later Japanese peasants started using karate, with their working tools as weapons, against Samurai warriors. All these skills were used to kill or maim opponents. I thank God I can now see the error of my ways.

I worked on many different building sites in my early twenties, bricklaying, plumbing and digging drains. Then I passed my heavy goods vehicle licence, so I could work all over Europe. I hadn't given God much thought for years, but I do believe He was with me all the time, protecting me. I was single and worked with a crowd of hard-drinking men, yet I didn't take any alcohol until I was 33. I never took drugs, though they were all the rage in the sixties.

At one time, through illness, I lived in "cardboard city" in London and had no money, yet I never went hungry. One day while working with a road gang, digging an underpass under a road, the foreman asked me to run an errand for him. As I walked away from the digging there was a mighty rumble and the hole caved in, killing five of my workmates.

Then one dark night I was driving a fully-laden 32-ton articulated lorry in Scotland and its back axle broke. The trailer shot off the road into a 6ft ditch and threw my cab into the air. It landed upside down in a field with me in it, yet I sustained only a few cuts and bruises. On many other occasions I could have been badly injured if not killed, but God saved me.

I spent the next four or five years moving around Europe with a trucking company and visited karate dojos in many countries. While there I met some Army personnel in karate competitions and became quite attached to them. We remained good friends and in one competition they asked if I would join their karate team. As this meant joining the Forces, I declined.

Two years later I met two of the team at another competition in England. By now we were all black belts and no longer took part in contests. We had all matured and I had married an Irish girl. My work kept me in England much of the time, but Ireland was my real home. After several meetings with my black-belted friends, I was told more about their team's activities and became very interested. Eventually I agreed to join them.

My training greatly intensified and now included

weaponry and survival. The next few years were filled with violence and danger and I am not proud of them, but that was what I was trained to do. Then there was an urgent telephone call; my wife was seriously ill in hospital with kidney failure. I rushed off to see her. As she lay dying, I watched her, wondering what life was all about. We had spent so much of our married life apart, but she was a good girl and I didn't think she deserved to die so young.

I left my unit five years later. Looking back, I wonder if any of it was necessary. During my final years in the Service I had the first signs of ME (myalgic encephalo-myelitis), though the doctors thought it was nervous tension and I certainly improved after I left the military and lived in England.

I then married my second wife. With her help I started my own plumbing and central heating business. Life was very good. We lived in the East End of London and had two daughters. But my illness gradually returned and someone suggested I visit a spiritualist healer. The desperate will try anything, so I went along.

To my surprise I started to feel a lot better, so I went for healing regularly. I also attended meetings and was invited to join a progressive circle. I thought I was doing well but my wife brought me back to reality. Our business was losing work with nothing coming in to replace it and my health deteriorated again.

As soon as we decided to leave the spiritualists our business began to recover. We had so much work we could not manage it all. But we were finding living in London more and more difficult. I spent hours in traffic jams while travelling to jobs and frequent problems finding parking spaces. We weren't happy with my elder daughter's school either. Christian assemblies were stopped after a huge influx of Muslims into the area.

Then one hot stifling summer about nine years ago the inner city riots started, so we decided to move out.

Freemasonry – a waste of time

Having settled in our present home in Kent, we had first to establish our business, so we advertised widely. One day, while picking up my supplies at a local merchant's, someone invited me to join the Freemasons. I talked this over with my wife and we concluded it could benefit the business, so, considering it an honour to have been asked, we went ahead. The ritual for joining the Lodge was very strange, as was that for each succeeding degree. They kept telling me I would enjoy the next part, but I never did. It all seemed a waste of time, though always with a promise of good times to come.

I was still going to the occasional meeting when my ME returned quite severely. It affected my back and legs and left me extremely weak. I could only work in the mornings, spending my afternoons in bed. My doctor confirmed that rest was the best treatment – but that didn't pay my bills! So I visited a chiropractor, whose manipulation really helped, but when I became very weak it was too harsh for me. I then tried a hypnotherapist and an acupuncturist and took the ground-up bark of an Amazonian tree, but none of these worked.

We were then introduced to a network marketing business by a couple who became our friends. One Saturday morning, while picking up our products at their house, they invited us to their church the next day. I said to my wife, "I think we're busy, aren't we darling?" But she replied, "No, I don't think we're doing anything. We'd love to come."

I was pleasantly surprised to find the church bursting at the seams, with a lovely noisy friendly atmosphere and loads of young people. We felt very welcome. When the choruses began, everyone was singing, clapping and dancing in the aisles and we really enjoyed ourselves.

I was listening to the Bible reading when a skinhead in front of me, covered in tattoos, wearing a leather jacket, earrings and bovver boots, turned round and handed me his Bible, open at the right page. I thanked him but shook my head in disbelief. We left that meeting bewildered. We had never seen people praise and worship our Lord Jesus with such enthusiasm.

After attending that church for a couple of months my health was still very poor, so our friends suggested we visit John Linden-Cook, who has a healing ministry in South London. I had only heard of spiritualist healing, but John uses the healing power of Jesus Christ. By now I was so desperate I would have tried anything to get pain relief.

Born again and healed!

We met John in May, 1991. I had imagined him taller and more commanding in stature – but then he started talking. What a sermon! As we sat in our seats I experienced such intense pain I found it very difficult to walk to the front of the hall to get born again. But I wanted to do it by my own effort. Having got there, I saw my wife beside me. "Thank You, Jesus!" I said to myself. John prayed with about 12 of us individually. When he came to me I accepted Jesus into my heart and felt such power that I nearly fell over. Much of my pain left me there and then.

When John called for those who needed healing, about half those there stood up and joined the queue. John took me aside so we could talk privately. I noticed the love and kindness shining from his face. I felt so unworthy of Jesus' love, particularly when John said after my confessions, "You haven't been a very nice man, have you?" But he assured me that if I would confess, renounce and repent of my sins, Jesus would love and forgive me.

I was delivered and healed by the power of Jesus and jumped up from the floor a new man. Bless You, Jesus! Praise Your Holy Name! I was so bursting with energy that my friend had to drive me home. I am now free from pain and don't need to rest in the afternoons. But more exciting than this, my wife and I have found Jesus. I now **know** that Jesus is the Son of God who came in the flesh to die for my sins on the Cross. I believe that God raised him from the dead and I know I'm saved.

Today we are members of a Community Church and have a wonderful friendship with our pastor and his wife, as well as the rest of the fellowship. We are learning so much from the Bible, which we read every day and thank God for such patient and understanding spiritual leaders.'

Chapter 14

A Quaker Healed of Osteomyelitis

'The dreaded bone disease osteomyelitis was once commonplace, but has become practically unknown in the UK since the late 1940s. I was one of the last to contract it as a teenager in 1942, just before antibiotics became generally available. As a result of that illness, I have had some 30 operations on my leg, six or seven on my arm and am deaf in one ear. To make matters worse, my leg broke under muscular contraction during the brittle stage of the illness. This shortened my leg and left some stiffness in my hip, giving me a small permanent limp. My legs slowly deteriorated after I had passed the peak of recovery from my original illness when I was 20, and both legs later became bent.

On the credit side, however, I am blessed with a wonderful Christian wife and a happy family life and continue to enjoy a career in high technology. Some seven years ago I gave my bad hip a knock while sledging with my children. It passed unnoticed, but probably triggered an osteomyelitis abscess, which accelerated the deterioration of my right leg and poisoned my whole system. I was troubled by pain in my legs, which started to affect my walking.

While at a dance in April, 1988, I could feel the cartilages moving in both my knees. Next month what I had long feared happened – something snapped in my right knee and I found I could not walk more than two or three paces without a stick.

In June the consultant delivered a devastating verdict. Looking at an old X-ray of my right knee, he said, "Your joint is shot to hell." Then, as I left, he added, "When the pain becomes unbearable, come and see me and we will talk about an operation." Osteomyelitis in the leg precludes knee or hip replacement, so that operation would have brought me considerable restriction and immobility. Another consultant confirmed the diagnosis of osteo-arthritis.

I did not give in. I tried various things to reverse the condition, but with only slight success. By January, 1989, I was in a bad way. Not only were both my legs affected, but my shoulders and elbow were becoming painful from using the stick. My sleep was disturbed by the pain. Crutches and eventually a wheelchair were in prospect and I expected my work to become limited to sitting at a computer terminal. Then, in that September, while in Germany, I was introduced to Full Gospel Business Men's Fellowship International by a German business colleague. He gave me some copies of the German edition of the Fellowship's magazine, *Stimme*, and some *Voice*, in English. When we returned home we contacted the Maidstone Chapter and Brenda and I enjoyed meetings there whenever I was home. While in Germany, I attended the Darmstadt Chapter meetings. Yet I did not seriously consider healing through prayer.

We were at the Maidstone Chapter Dinner on 1st February, 1989, when John Linden-Cook was the guest speaker, not realising it would be a healing meeting. Anyway we knew virtually nothing about miraculous healing. At the end, the President said that John, who had described many healing miracles during his testimony, would pray for healing for anyone who wanted it.

Not ready – but the Lord was!

Brenda urged me to go for prayer, but I resisted, saying that I was not ready. However, a lady we had talked with over the dinner came to me and said, "God has told me that you must go to John." So, with bad grace, I agreed and late that evening I asked John to pray for me. As we prayed, he said, "In the name of Jesus Christ I rebuke the spirit of arthritis in Sydney!" I felt nothing and, as it was nearly midnight, we left the meeting.

Outside, Brenda stopped and looked at me. I knew she expected me to try to walk without my stick. I had painfully dragged myself the 100 yards from my car into the meeting with the help of my stick and I knew I could manage three or four paces at most without a stick. Well, I was wrong! Limping heavily and out of breath, I was yet able to walk the 100 yards back to the car **without** my stick – **and** without pain!

That night I enjoyed my first pain-free rest in months. The next day when I got up, I made short trial walks around the house without my stick, thrilled that there was no pain. Then I had the curious feeling that the heel of my shortened leg dragged on the ground as I walked. Going upstairs, I removed some clothes and looked in the long bedroom mirror. I could not believe what I saw, so I called Brenda. After careful examination, turning this way and that, we agreed that the right leg was no longer bent but straight. It had changed while I was asleep.

Since then the improvement has continued slowly but steadily, with the occasional setback. To start with I kept my stick with me while away from home, as I lacked confidence. But as my leg muscles strengthened and my circulation improved, I was able to walk further and further without it. Finally, that April I used my stick for the last time and returned it to the hospital. In September I asked my GP for an appointment with a physiotherapist to help me recover from osteo-arthritis. He is impressed with my progress, of course. On one occasion I walked as much as three miles.

My marriage, which was already good, has now become far better as a result of my healing, and the effects on my spiritual life have been tremendous. People say that I look much better and I am convinced that the original chronic osteomyelitis has gone for good. I believe this gift of healing has come to me from the Lord Jesus Christ. I believe it is vital to know the source of one's healing, as healing involves a commitment.

I delayed writing this testimony because my healing is ongoing and my legs are still in an "uncertain" state, though I am appreciably better than I was some months ago. Then my healing has shaken me up fundamentally. The straightening of my deformed bones was quite beyond my understanding, and I still think of it with wonder, though I carry the evidence around with me. As a Quaker I was totally ignorant about healing by prayer. A week or two after my healing, I went to my GP to find out what could possibly change the shape of a leg. I also stood in front of my mirror on several occasions, twisting my leg this way and that and trying to put it into its original position. I could not, because it had changed shape!

The slight but permanent limp that resulted from my original illness has also gone. This further confirms that my femur has changed shape and a strong hint that the chronic osteomyelitis has finally gone. After my healing I was totally free from pain in all eight affected joints for about 10 days, with one puzzling exception – my left elbow. A day or two later I realised that the pain was not in the joint but in a strained muscle – perhaps tennis elbow? – caused by walking with a stick.

I feel it is vital that people who have been prayed for for healing should be told that the after-effects of healing can often resemble the original pains. This certainly happens when healing is by conventional means and it happened to me after my healing through prayer. I experienced all sorts of muscle pains, burning pains from a re-expanding circulatory system and itchy sensations in my formerly arthritic joints.

After 10 days, some of the pains temporarily returned. If I had not remained positive about my healing, I might well have lost it. But Brenda helped me to keep positive. To be very practical, persistent limping on a normal leg would have undone the good that had been achieved. So most of the pains that followed my healing were healing pains.'

Chapter 15

An Alcoholic Delivered

'I had been 25 years a Christian when I developed a severe menopausal problem, accompanied by depression. Though menopausal problems tend to be laughed at, they can cause havoc as the hormones become out of balance. As soon as one symptom clears up, another appears. To ease the tension I started drinking – a little at first, but later I could not stop.

I soon found alcoholism is insatiable and wants the whole of you. It is as cruel as the grave, affecting not only the body, but – far worse – the mind. I believe it is one of Satan's deadliest weapons, as it totally destroys its victim. Under the influence of drink you do many things you would not otherwise dream of doing – lying, cheating, stealing, among others. It completely changes one's personality until you have no control of yourself at all.

I got in such a state that I tried three times to commit suicide. After one attempt I was in an Intensive Care Unit and my husband was not sure whether I was going to live or die. To think of taking your own life is a violation of God's law, but life becomes so unbearable, like a living hell, that I felt I could take no more.

The alcoholic's first downward step is to lose his or her job. I did, after 28 years in a responsible position with a missionary society. Next, you lose your partner and family. I nearly lost my husband, Mike, as he had had just about all he could take. It was affecting him badly in various ways and living with an alcoholic is an horrific experience. My family do not live near me, so I was able to hide it from them.

Then, thirdly, you lose your friends. Fortunately, those of mine who knew about my affliction stood by me, prayed for me, counselled me and some of them laid hands on me. My GP also laid hands on me at least three times in his surgery. I eventually agreed to go into hospital for my alcoholism, but that did not help. I came out, still desperate and thought I was losing my sanity.

Then there was my guilt. I was so ashamed of what I had become and how I had let God and everybody else down. My Christian doctor helped me to accept God's forgiveness. (I knew all the relevant texts, but it was extremely difficult to accept them for myself.) His non-Christian partner helped me to forgive myself, which proved harder than accepting God's forgiveness, as I felt so vile, degraded and worthless.

I usually had only two hours sleep a night, despite taking sleeping tablets. I used to lie there, wondering what the future held and how, if ever, I would hold down a job. I knew the Lord was my only answer, but I did not know what He was going to do or when. I dreaded each day – even more, the nights.

When a friend wanted to go to a healing service held by the Norwood Christian Fellowship, I went with her, though I had not heard of them before. I did not know whether to go forward for healing, as hands had been laid on me so many times. But my husband said, "What harm can it do?" So, being at my wits' end, I went forward but was not healed at that time. Puzzled at this, I phoned John who explained that God does not always heal immediately, sometimes it took time. He suggested that I went again, so I did and again had hands laid on me.

I did not feel noticeably different after this, but the next day I was restless. I got up at 2 am and started to re-read *I'm Sold on Being Bold* by Don Gossett, which a friend had lent me. My healing came gradually as I studied that book and I have not looked back since that day, 2nd September, 1984.

They told me that my mind had been severely damaged by the drink. In fact, my psychiatrist told me he had never met anyone whose mind had been so badly ravaged after drinking for such a short time. He gave me only five years to live if I continued drinking – ten at the most. Once vibrant and full of confidence, I became just the opposite.

Body and soul healed

My mind is now fine, my confidence has returned and, best of all, I have no desire for drink. The menopausal problem has cleared up too. I look forward to living each new day. It is exciting! After taking a full-time refresher Secretarial Course, I am now doing temp work and two firms have asked for my name and address so they can take me on if a permanent vacancy crops up. It is a miracle! I cannot praise Jesus and thank Him enough for healing me and giving me back my mind and my body.

I realised afterwards that He could not heal me until I had surrendered **everything** to Him. I had struggled against this for a long time. What a fool! If I had surrendered earlier, I am sure I would have been healed sooner. Folk now say I am back to my old self, but I claim it is a **different** me. I have now yielded myself totally to Him and want Jesus Christ to have full control of my life.

My relationship with Jesus is more real now. He is everything to me. I stand amazed – and so thankful – at the way Jesus loves me and for healing me – and for Mike staying with me and putting up with so much. I shall never be able to repay him. Also for all the wonderful people who stood by me, loving me in spite of what I had become. This astounds and humbles me, as they did not **have** to bother.

I do not know why God had to let this nightmare overtake me, but the experience has certainly brought me to a closer and far better relationship with Jesus and is also helping me to understand and help other people. My healing has encouraged many others. I give all praise, honour and glory to the Lord Jesus Christ, for I know that "I am my Beloved's and my Beloved is mine".'

Chapter 16

'Alice in Wonderland'

On one occasion I was invited to be the main speaker at the Salisbury Chapter of the Full Gospel Business Men's Fellowship International and I still have vivid memories of that evening and its sequel. I was met at the station by the then President, John Bryant, and taken to the hotel where the dinner was being held. It was a room in the style of an Elizabethan Hall with oak panelling and cross-beams, altogether quite an attractive venue. There were quite a large number of people there and we all enjoyed a good meal. The evening proceeded in the normal way for a Chapter Dinner. After I had spoken several came forward for salvation and were prayed for. Then the sick were called forward and during this time a father came forward with his 12-year-old daughter. She was suffering from muscular dystrophy and could not walk – he had half-carried her forward. She was my idea of Alice in Wonderland, blonde hair down to her shoulders, very prettily dressed and she had lovely blue eyes – these I was to remember in the days ahead.

Her father told me what her problem was. I prayed for her rebuking the spirit of muscular dystrophy and commanding it to leave her in Jesus' name. On opening my eyes after the prayer and looking down at her I was grieved to see the look on her face. That one look said it all – 'what a pity it didn't work' she seemed to be saying to me although she never actually spoke. I said to her, 'I want you to thank the Lord Jesus for healing you. You are to do that for the next week. Will you do that?' Her head nodded in obedience and I looked at her father and said, 'will you see that she does that?' His reply was short and very firm, 'she will.' With that he took her back to where they had been sitting. The evening continued with prayer for those who needed it and we departed to John's house where I was to stay the night. That was on the Monday. On the Saturday of that week I was working in the garden when Elsa came out and said that John Bryant from Salisbury was on the phone and wanted to speak to me. As I hurried into the house I noticed that it was just 4 pm, a time that has meant a great deal to me since for it was then I heard the good news.

John and I exchanged greetings and then he said, 'Do you remember the little blonde girl on Monday night who couldn't walk?' 'Yes,' I replied, 'Her face has haunted me ever since.' 'Well,' John said, 'I've waited until now because I wanted to make sure it was true. She has been running around the garden and playing with her friends since Thursday.' I was overjoyed. Some nine years later I went to the Salisbury Chapter again, this time to take a teaching day. I wondered if I would see her. However, this was not to be, but I was told that she was now a ladies hairdresser. Regretfully she had to work that Saturday afternoon and that there was nothing wrong with her. Her healing was permanent. Praise the Lord.

Miracles at Inverness

Another story concerning a young girl happened when I visited the Inverness Chapter of the FGBMFI. The meeting followed the usual pattern of a Chapter Dinner and there were many people who came forward to be born again that night. After this we prayed for those who needed healing. A 15-year-old girl came forward with a problem we had not encountered before. She had great difficulty in breathing which meant it was difficult for her to walk upstairs and playing games was out. We prayed for her and cast out this spirit of infirmity and she collapsed on the floor dead to the world. After a few minutes she sat up on the floor and began to cry – or was it to laugh? It turned out she was doing both – her breathing was now so much easier but not completely normal. I asked her to thank the Lord Jesus for healing her and setting her free and she went off.

The following year I was again invited to speak at the Inverness Chapter. This young lady, who was the grand-daughter of the President, was asked to give her testimony of what had happened on my previous visit. She related her problem and of how much easier it had been to breathe after I had prayed for her. The night following the dinner she had been preparing to go to Guides when she told her mother that she felt somewhat sick. Her mother wisely told her to go and be sick. This she did and the last of the infirmity left her and her breathing was normal. It was at the same dinner a young man related how I had prayed for him the previous year and that he had been healed of ME. How gracious our God is.

Chapter l7

Three Short Testimonies

Body odour banished

'Towards the end of 1992 I attended an FGBMFI meeting in West London at which John Linden-Cook gave an address on healing and deliverance and ministered to a number of people including me.

Some months earlier I had been given a promise, which I believed to be from God, to the effect that God would heal my hurts.

One of these was quite severe acne. This did not affect my everyday life directly, but affected me psychologically. The other was BO which I could not eradicate and which afflicted me particularly at work. It had been so disruptive to my working relationships that I had felt obliged to leave my first job and join another firm. There it played a large part in losing me that job also.

At the FGBMFI meeting I hesitated for a long time before going forward, not because I doubted that I could be healed but mainly because I was embarrassed. However, I did go forward and was very relieved when John had the sensitivity to draw me to one side and whisper, "Get out, you spirit of BO." He also prayed for my acne. Others ministered to me for deliverance from a spirit of grief and a spirit of rejection. It was an extremely emotional experience.

The next morning I awoke with an involuntary cry and over the next four days I could smell the odour rolling off my clothes and personal possessions. This problem of BO has not troubled me since.

Some months later I fell in love and got married. My acne has improved, particularly since getting married and I am confident that it will eventually be healed totally.'

The spirit of the bull

Earlier we mentioned a teaching day which I had undertaken for the Salisbury Chapter. There was a young man there who asked for prayer because he was subject to suddenly being very violent. The Chapter members prayed for him during the ministry time but they felt unable to cope with the situation and asked me to go and help. Firstly, I asked him to confess, renounce and repent of this and to tell the spirit of violence to leave him and this he did with startling results. He started to fight and some five of the men there tried to hold him. I commanded the spirit of the bull to leave him and then told the men to just let go of him. As he was a few inches off the floor at the time he fell down and at that moment the spirit left him and as far as I know it has never returned. Praise the Lord who is Victor in all things.

A modern Mary of Magdala

Here is an excerpt from a letter we recently received from someone we ministered to some years ago:

'Fornication and adultery had become part of my life-style, but through the deliverance ministry of the NCF the Lord Jesus Christ set me free from a spirit of harlotry and other demons and I was born again.

By God's mercy these demons did not get back in again. From early childhood I practised masturbation, a sex perversion. I continued with this for many years as an adult, even when a sex partner was available. At times I longed to give it up, along with my whole rotten life-style, but the habit had me bound. It had become a necessity of living.

But praise the Lord, when I was born again at the Norwood Christian Fellowship meeting some months ago, the need left me at once. Jesus Christ and His will immediately became all-important to me, for I am so grateful for His sacrifice for me.

"It is no longer I who live, but Christ lives in me."
(Galatians 2:20)

Rejoicing in my freedom, I am writing this to tell all who will read it that nothing is impossible with God.

Life is glorious now. I rejoice in the one Lord – my Lord – who loved me enough to die a horrible death for me, shedding His Blood to cleanse me and set me free! Thank you, John and Elsa, for ministering the love of Jesus to me. Above all, thank you Jesus, for setting me free.'

Chapter 18

Condemned to a Life of Pain

'I was born in Mysore (Southern India) as a Hindu. My family for generations were religious God-fearing people, who were strict vegetarians. The prayer room, kitchen and dining room were out of bounds to people of other religions and faiths. Even I was considered unclean to go and eat in the dining room if I had gone to a house where they ate meat. Because of the very orthodox environment and traditions of man-made holiness, I resented some customs even from an early age and refused to observe certain customs for tradition's sake.

I was born with a deformity to both my legs. In a Mission Hospital called Holdsworth Memorial Hospital my mother offered me back to the Creator and said either God who is a good God will heal my son or take him back and save him from being mocked and teased all his life. So I was operated upon and put in knee-length iron shoes to correct the deformity. I never crawled for I was in shoes for nearly $2\frac{1}{2}$ years. My prayer was, "Almighty God, protect me – give me a good education, good clothes and good health and keep me safe."

In the morning and in the evening I thanked Him for helping me and looking after me.

I did this for over 20 years. God, I believe, gave me wisdom and insight, for way back in early 1950 I had this desire birthed in me to become an electrical engineer. So I did my BSc in engineering, which taught me to respect abstract power with great discipline. Any breaking of the laws meant instant death. For I was dealing with very high voltage transmission lines like 220,000 volts and huge step-up and step-down transformers.

Then I joined the Air Force as a Commissioned Officer. Here I learnt authority when I was the duty officer. Even officers who did not obey the Station Rules could be punished by a junior officer like myself – and at the same time even a corporal could make one "run" as a punishment for not polishing one's shoes, or brass buttons on our uniforms.

I then went into farming – there I learnt about weeds, fertilisers – patience and seasons. Long hard days of bringing new fields into cultivation brought very little in the initial years – but as the soil got richer the crops were yielding better quality corn. I also learnt the importance of watering, till in the end one could look after the crops for 90 days very diligently, yet how, if neglected for three or four days, the yield could so easily be reduced by 15–20%. I also learnt about the power of God as transformer of a caterpillar to a moth, by rearing silkworms from a tiny egg in under 25 days of growth to be about $3-3\frac{1}{2}$ inches long and then turning into a beautiful moth.

Then I turned direction towards computers, and learnt the art of making the machine do what I wanted it to do – then progressed to design and implementing systems to match clients' needs.

Whilst playing badminton I tore my knee ligaments

and cartilage in 1963 – which resulted in cortisone injections. I played many sports. I was in pain 24 hours a day, seven days a week. I suppose due to my early pain of operations as a baby, it had lifted me to a higher level of "pain threshold". Doctors could not promise recovery and only condemned me to a life of pain with arthritis to follow.

Arrogance and pride

I came to England in 1971 and worked for many computer firms. In 1979, at the peak of my career, "I hit the deck" hard due to my own arrogance and pride. I was being introduced to some very famous people as a very bright outstanding computer systems programmer.

In 1982 I was invited to a FGBMFI Meeting at the Café Royal by a colleague called Ken White. I was so dead to the work of God, not one word meant anything to me. However, in June 1982 I gave my life to the Lord at the Café Royal. The following morning a sincere gentleman by the name of Barry encouraged me to visit him for prayer. He prayed prayers (which I never quite understood at the time) but now I know were prayers for idolatry, occult etc. I owe a great deal to Barry for his loving support in many ways. He took me on a trip to France – which changed my whole attitude to God.

I saw the reality of a living God manifesting His power to deliver, heal and comfort people. This quickened my desire to walk with God.

At an FGBMFI meeting in the Oaklands Park Hotel there were about 150 people and a speaker called John Linden-Cook. He said among other things, "God wants to heal three specific conditions. Will they please respond to these: (1) a person with kidney problems, (2) a person with migraine, (3) a person with a painful leg." He persisted on the leg. He said the problem was not the ankle. I felt I needed more specific direction to respond. I have searched my heart and I can truly say that God put the thought into my heart that He was not a teaser or a mocker – His power and integrity were unquestionable. So I was waiting for God to do more before I could respond. Then John said it appears not to be the hip; he stayed on it for a considerable time. Still I was not able to respond – then he said it appears to be between the ankle and the hip. I felt my hope and expectation rising within me – but still I was looking about to see if anyone else was responding to the call. No one got up – and finally John said, "It is the left leg more like the knee." Then I got up and started walking towards him. While I was still about six feet away from him he pointed a finger at me and said, "You are the one with a bad painful leg, aren't you?" I was surprised but never took much note of it for this was all new to me. He prayed and to be absolutely honest I never felt anything, but this thought – that God never mocks – went over and over in my mind and I decided to try it out the next night by playing a game of squash with a friend, with whom I had not played for nearly $2\frac{1}{2}$ years. I nearly always won against him in the past – so he was delighted that finally he had the opportunity to get his own back. I started very gingerly but felt no pain and began to stretch, and finally played a match and beat him. No doubt he was most upset, but I was delighted that the pain of 10 years had finally gone.

What God does lasts

I believe God delivers us to serve Him in newness of life and understanding with a grateful heart. What He does lasts. God is not a temporary fixer. I have kept my wholeness and healing for over 10 years and can truly say, "God is a good God." He is good all the time when we walk humbly with Him. There is no room for pride or arrogance because God hates it and any indulgence in these things incurs His wrath.

I bless the saints who have so faithfully given their time to travel miles, and spent time to seek God's face, and then been bold to speak out not fearing the consequences of such an action. All this takes a lot of time and single-mindedness which is often hardly understood or appreciated by most people. His word says God is the rewarder of all who obey Him and labour in His work. I can truly now say that Jesus makes the difference and there is none better or equal to Him. He alone is worthy of our love, praise, worship and adoration. He is deeply concerned for our well-being all the time.

I would like to say that no gardener puts weeds on his own lawn – yet the weeds grow regularly which need weeding to keep the garden clean. Likewise we have to "weed out" from our hearts the things that displease God. As we live in a polluted world we cannot be but affected by it, but with loving brothers and sisters like John and Elsa who have been a great blessing to me and to my family in helping us to do the "weeding" and without any reservation, we freely acknowledge that our lives have been sweetened by their willingness and obedience to God's love.'

Chapter 19

Satan's 'Little Princess'?

In the church in South London we had met Ginger. She very obviously disliked us very much. She refused to talk to us. When we insisted on her answering a simple question, she used to turn her back on us, then her face turned sideways and we got a short answer, quite clearly saying with it, 'Leave me alone!'

We had met many troubled people, but no one like this. We sometimes said to her, 'Praise the Lord, you did answer us,' which was acknowledged with an unfriendly grunt. Much later on she told us that the voices in her had said to her: 'Have nothing to do with these people.'

We learned something about her background. Her mother seemed to have been involved in a local coven, but she described it as 'spiritism'. Her grandmother had also been very involved and some of the members of her mother's family.

The vicar of that church had tried to pray with her, but found he could not find enough time to deal with her problems, which were many. So one evening he asked us to pray with her. This is what Ginger said about the vicar's suggestion:

'I had arranged to have prayer with the vicar one Saturday night and turned up, shaking in my shoes as usual with fear and apprehension. We went through to the church and to my horror who should be waiting there for me but the couple I had avoided like the plague. The vicar had not told me they would be there as he had guessed I would not then have turned up. To make matters worse, he then told me he was leaving me with them and would be back later. There was no escape! They started to minister to me and, as I found out later, all hell seemed to break loose. I realised that my mother had been deeper into the realms of darkness than I was aware. The vicar returned shortly after and I went home. Next day I told him that I never wanted to have prayer with that couple again.

In the next few days a lady, who was very kind to me, came with them to church. She shared with me what the Lord Jesus had done for her through them. It was some time later that I began to realise they were not as bad as I had thought. I knew I had to apologise to them for being rude to them. So I did and was then more or less at peace with them!'

We now were greeted by Ginger in a happier way – but still she did not look at us and stayed well away from us. Also whenever she came near us she seemed to have 'overactivity' in her finger muscles. They twitched frantically – even in her pockets – and her thumb was chewed to the flesh. Now Ginger again:

'The Lord then began to suggest that I should ask them to pray for me, but I dismissed the idea. A few weeks later though, I changed my mind and

156

decided to ask them. Soon after Christmas 1970 I was very scared during a healing service. They were there, but as the fog had come down, they had left promptly at the end of the service. I was in such a state by then. I could not control it. I knew that if I did not ask them for prayer that night, I would not be able to do so later. So I plucked up courage, got their telephone number and rang them. When they answered I nearly dropped the phone.'

It was after 10 pm that Saturday when our 'phone rang. I lifted the receiver – there was no answer. Then I heard a small voice – 'Please would you pray for me . . .' silence. I turned to John and told him who it was. We both felt that this was the hand of the Lord Jesus. Ginger was in His special care and He had given her the courage to ring us. So we told her that we would see her the next day to make arrangements. The next day we said that we would be pleased to see her and to come along the following Monday.

We were very blessed living in a detached house. One of the upstairs rooms we had set apart as a prayer room – partly a bedroom, with a couch, a small wardrobe, an armchair, two other chairs, a small table and a wash-basin. On the table stands a small wooden cross, on the wall above the table we have a print showing a painting by S. Dali. Eleven men are kneeling in an upper room round a big table, all in European dress. On the table are the bread and wine. The artist painted the Lord Jesus being above it with His arms outstretched, though not in an earthly body but in His resurrection body. In the background are the lake and fishing boats on it. For us it reminds us of the reality of the Lord's presence when we confess our sins and eat the bread and drink the wine, as He commanded us to do. We do this whenever we pray casting out evil spirits, counsel people and pray for healing of hurtful memories.

Ginger:

> 'We went to their Prayer Room and had – oh! no, not Communion surely! But yes it was, and I was in deep trouble by then. I just about managed to take the bread and the wine, then I passed out. I was actually unaware of what I was saying. The evil spirits in me were speaking and manifesting their evil ways and powers through my mouth and body.'

We were glad that Ginger had managed to come to our house. We were told by her that a young lady from Operation Mobilisation had talked to her about giving her heart to the Lord and Ginger said she had done that with this lady. We said to Ginger that we were glad that she knew the Lord Jesus because then she would be happy to kneel down before the little cross and say 'Praise the Lord.' Suddenly a strong voice shouted – **"Never!"** and Ginger was rolling on the floor.

We realised that we were dealing with the deep things of Satan. This was not an ordinary problem of demon trouble, we were facing a legion of evil spirits! The demons were very strong, shouting abuse at us, trying to kill her with her own hands, spitting and scratching us. So we stopped. We bound the spirits and commanded them to stop manifesting. Then we talked to Ginger and asked her to say a prayer of repentance and renounce Satan and his forces. Though this young lady had a junior job in an office she could not say 'I repent' or 'Jesus'.

We realised then that the demons had ground in her because of unconfessed sins. So we battled on for half an hour, probably more than that, encouraging her to say 'I repent of all my sins. Jesus forgive me.' In the end she managed to say these words, very slowly. It seemed to us that something else was saying the words. We encountered that again whenever she confessed and renounced sins. She sounded like a child speaking. It may have been her mind only, but there was no heart meaning to it. Therefore we felt there was no true repentance. But we had to leave it at that.

Ginger:

'During some time of prayer ministry I remember being terribly frightened. I saw what had happened to me as a baby. I know this will be very difficult to understand but I will do my best to explain it. I saw people that I knew from my childhood all dressed in black. I also saw the table where I was laid as a baby and things that were done to me. I was absolutely terrified. I remember clinging on to John and crying bitterly. This vision lasted quite a while. The Lord healed my memories through His love. I can now look at this part of the trauma without hate or fear.

I have mentioned earlier about my mother's and grandmother's involvement in the occult. The Lord showed us that I needed to repent of all their occult practices, as the Lord God still visits on the children the iniquities of their forefathers up to the fourth generation of them that hated Him. I understood that as I was of the flesh and bones of my forefathers, I had part of their dark deeds. But if I asked the Lord Jesus to wash me clean from these iniquities I would be blessed. John explained to me that as I had to go to the Lord Jesus to have my sins forgiven so I had to ask Him to wash me clean from the occult sins of my forefathers. I found this

159

very difficult to do for I considered my involvement very small; I used to read my horoscopes and was superstitious. I repented of that. But to repent of the iniquities of my forefathers was tremendously difficult. I would get about three or four words out and then collapse. This happened a few times. Then John again rebuked the powers of darkness who were stopping me from doing this, and I got on a bit better although it was still very difficult.'

Ginger was greatly blessed after this prayer time. We learned that to dislodge the ground on which evil spirits were sitting, repentance and renunciation were necessary. We then added prayer for the healing of hurtful memories and found that more evil spirits left quickly.

Sometimes Ginger stayed with us over a weekend. One evening when we were having a time of prayer and thanksgiving a voice started to shout at us. We were surprised at the ordinary human way of speech. It was ugly and commanding. It insisted it had a right to be in Ginger. It claimed to be Ginger's grandmother! That lady had died shortly after Ginger had been born. Ginger had not been aware of this, so we told her what had happened.

Ginger:

'Before I was born my mother fell down almost a full flight of stairs which was the beginning of my troubles, as I think that incident let in spirits of fear. My mother at that time was attending seances and was also "prayed" for by the medium. I was born after a great deal of trouble with the birth. I was born 3–4 weeks later than I should have been and my skin was burned from lack of birth water. The midwife who was present told my mother they would never raise me and she just put me in the cot to die. Soon after I was born my grandmother took me to a spiritist as I was so poorly. I think it was promised that if I lived I would be given to Satan as his child. At the age of four months I was taken to a satanic meeting, baptized to Satan and given to him in a blood covenant ceremony. I still have a small cut on the small finger of my right hand that has not completely disappeared after 40 odd years!'

That strong voice shouted again and it did not obey the command to leave in the Name of the Lord Jesus. We cried to the Lord to send his angels to deliver Ginger from this ugly manifestation.

We woke Ginger out of her trance and told her about the voice speaking again. We helped Ginger to speak forcefully and withdraw the permission given to this being to enter her so long ago. It was not easy for her to say it. We witnessed after that the most amazing voices, shouting and screaming, and Ginger's body was shaking from head to toe. Then there was peace. We asked the Holy Spirit to fill that space this 'thing' had occupied. Ginger was very glad, for something awful had left her. We wondered, was it really a human spirit, the spirit of her grandmother? or a very powerful spirit that had dwelt in her grandmother? Why did it not obey the command in the Name of Jesus to leave? But it went when we asked the Lord to send His angels and evict this spirit.

On another occasion we had a manifestation that was cast out after we called to the Lord Jesus to send His angels. It was a very powerful spirit, which described itself as the angel of the covenant of death. We broke the covenant of death that must have been made by her or on her behalf early in her life.

Ginger:

'I remember as I grew up I was terrified of all animals and of dogs especially. If I was out and wanted to go home and there was a dog where I had to go, I would do a long detour to avoid it. I would even ring my father and ask him to come and meet me, which he always did. I was also terrified of thunderstorms and would be physically sick when one was brewing up. Once it had actually started I would try and find somewhere to hide – anywhere that was dark. I almost had hysterics. As the Lord Jesus delivered me of my legion of fears I noticed a great change in my attitude to cats and dogs. John and Elsa acquired a (rescue) dog, a lovely cocker spaniel. I amazed my family talking about this pet and one day my mother came to visit us and the dog was staying with us as John and Elsa were on holiday. She could hardly believe her eyes. But her reaction was, she must have grown out of it. I gave her a copy of Raphael Gasson's book *The Challenging Counterfeit* but she showed no interest in it. Though she must have known the root of my many problems she would not talk about it.'

Several years had gone by since we had that 'phone call that Saturday evening, and a small voice had asked to come for prayer. Ginger was a very different young lady. Her face had changed, it was much softer, and she had some healing of her leg which seemed to be shorter than the other. Often we had a good time of fellowship, and she attended our prayer meetings and Bible study evenings faithfully.

She had experienced being attacked by evil spirits in

the street, or on an Underground station. Often a voice told her to throw herself in front of the Underground train. She also had the same experience when she stood at the top of an escalator, and there were occasions when a strange force pushed her down, once off a bus, once down concrete steps. She used to stand with her back to the wall at the Underground station, then she stopped going by Underground trains. There were spirits of death, destruction and murder in her, and slowly she was delivered from them.

In spite of these problems Ginger was now a good audio typist and a good secretary to her boss. She was very different, she seemed to have grown up. The evil spirits may have blocked her from developing normally. She had forgiven the group of people and her mother who had caused her much unhappiness. We have learned that it is very important to forgive all those that have wronged us and ask the Lord Jesus to bless these people. A wonderful freedom then comes into our hearts. Ginger had bought a 3-bedroomed house with a friend of hers, another young Christian lady. One Sunday morning we were going to see them and enjoy a cup of coffee with them, when Ginger said, 'I am not really sure whether I am truly born again. I don't seem to be as secure in the love of the Lord Jesus as you and the other members of the Fellowship are.' She had been taught that by being baptised and confirmed in the Church of England she had obtained eternal life. We also had baptised her in our bath, hoping that this would help her to gain deliverance from the remaining evil spirits. It was a blessing to her, but she was still not free from bondage. Then the end of the battle was in sight. The Lord had given Ginger a revelation. She put it down on paper in a letter to us, and this is what she wrote:

'Sunday night: I was seeing what I think was the last ceremony that I took part in – couldn't get it out of my mind. I really did try. I felt so dirty and unclean that is why I wanted to go, especially when we sang, "Be still for the presence of the Lord is here".

I know at that last ceremony it was Halloween night and I think that I did things that I am not sure if I have repented of. I know that I killed at least one baby and because of all the frenzy that the people were getting into I was really enjoying it. It appalled me last night because I could see myself being praised for killing the babies and that there was another ceremony that they did to me. I think it was something really bad because every time I try to recall it I can't, but even writing this is difficult. I know that there cannot be anything worse than killing a baby but I know there is. I think this is the last baby that I killed. I had to drink some of the blood and then it was taken away and there is an awful smell that I can smell while I am writing this like burning flesh. Then a bit later on something is brought in and I have to eat something. I am scared, very scared now. It is the baby I have killed. O Lord this is too awful!

I know what I have to write is true. I could smell that smell last night and it was as if I was in a trance most of the evening and I was reliving that last night. I could see the blood on my hands and it was the blood of that little one. I was given special praise that night. They are all dancing around me and then the sex starts again. So many times my heart is racing just to write this down. O Lord, help me, please. I believe that there were other sacrifices, before I had to kill the baby, that were going on.

164

There were young children there and the other men and women were having sex on and off all the evening. The baby I killed was born that night. They said that the baby was for me, it was to be my baby. Why oh why did I have to kill it? Why? I don't know the answer.

I know that I am born again and believe in Jesus. I do Satan, I do.

The baby's father was the chief man of the coven. I think that the baby's spirit came into me when I killed it there and I believe the baby's father is still alive and has a hold on me through all of this.

Whilst writing this I am seeing it all again as I have never seen anything before. This is worse than what I saw when I was with you both before.

I know that I have not confessed, renounced or repented of these things and I believe that is why I had the problem last night. Somehow that baby that I killed and her father have a hold in my life.

The words are coming back to me. Oh Lord help me to remember them, please . . .

"You have done well, little princess. On you are bestowed all the gifts of our sovereign master. You are now part of us, you belong to us. You are our treasured possession and you have done well, princess. You will be mighty in our beloved kingdom; you are a true vessel for us. You have power to do what you will. You are truly one of us, little princess, bound to us with invisible cords. You are mine, little princess."

There is a figure that just seems to come from the floor. It is Satan, I know it is. He looks like the man in black at the bottom of your bed that I saw when I

165

was staying with you in your guest bedroom. He takes me in his arms and it is as if he is blessing me. I am passed around and kissed and cuddled and made a big fuss of. I feel so powerful as if I could do anything. The people are in such a frenzy. There are goats and chickens there, their throats are cut, there is dancing again and sex again. A figure rapes me. I am suddenly very afraid and he knows it. He gives me back to the thing that came from the floor and he takes me in his arms and tells me not to be afraid, he will always be with me. I have something wrong with my arms and legs. I tell him and he uses something on my right and left legs and my left arm and hand, he says that the pain is gone and I feel better again. He gives me back to the father of the baby and says there is your new daughter, a true child of our kingdom. Thank you Jesus for reminding me and helping me. Please hold me and set me free from this evil.

I feel so ice cold now that I have finished typing this. I know that all this is true and I believe that the Lord Jesus has shown it to me.'

We suggested to her to go before the Lord Jesus and write down all the sins she could remember, right back to her school days, which were traumatic to her. She was even, as a young child of 11 years old, treated with ECT – a frightening experience for her. She had some involvement with boyfriends in her teens which resulted in an abortion. This was done against her will. She was overruled by her parents and doctors. She was not considered balanced enough emotionally to have a child. Later on in her life she was comforted by the statement of one of the evil spirits that this baby was to have been for their use. She was glad that it had not been born.

Ginger faithfully wrote down all the sins that she could remember. There were about three typewritten sheets full of them. We asked her to come into our prayer room. She knelt down and quietly read her confession to the Lord Jesus. We did not listen to it. At the end John gave her absolution and told her that as she had confessed to the Lord so He had forgiven her. He had not only forgiven her, He had forgotten them. We told the evil spirits that they had no more ground in Ginger for she had confessed all her sins and repented of them. She had renounced the devil and all his works and she had forgiven all the people that had used her and caused her so much heartache. Then the evil spirits were commanded to leave. We addressed them as familiar spirits, spirit of destruction, spirit of death and spirit of Satan. They seemed to go quickly except for the last one. John thinks it would be helpful if he gave you a run-down on this final ministry. This last spirit was now very weak, no more shouting and defying us, no longer were there any threats to kill her before it went, no longer was it manifesting violently as on so many occasions. But it did not go.

Elsa once again asked this spirit its name to which it replied in a very quiet but firm voice, 'Satan.' 'Satan, what?' said Elsa. 'What is your second name?' 'Satan.' 'And you've not been told to go?' asked Elsa, adding 'but you have been told to go.' 'No,' said the spirit. 'Yes, you have,' we replied. **'No.'** 'What do you mean "No"?' I asked. 'I haven't been told to go.' I hit the roof, as they say. 'The one that has just spoken to us and said, "I haven't been told to go", I now tell you to go in Jesus Christ's name. Now get out! Leave!' This brought results! There was a lot of screaming and then silence. Ginger herself told this spirit to leave her and there was another bout of screaming. After this Ginger said that she had experienced nothing like that before. We told Ginger that the spirit had told us just before the screaming that the others had all gone and that he had given his name as Satan. It had indeed been a frightening experience for her with physical manifestations in her tummy and throat.

Ginger now commanded Satan to leave and took away the permission given him to enter her. She claimed the blood of Jesus for her cleansing and the spirit began to manifest itself by heavy breathing. It was at this point that the final battle began.

We said, 'Satan, we address you in the name of the living God, Jesus Christ, and we adjure you in His name to come out. You have been told by Ginger (here we gave her full name) to leave. She has taken away the permission given you to enter in the first place. That is now rescinded and annulled by the blood of Jesus which she claimed. Therefore you have no longer any legal right to remain. Therefore, Satan, I exorcise you in the name of the Church, the Father, the Son, and the Holy Spirit and I command Satan to leave. Be exorcised in Jesus' Name. Go, Satan. Ginger (using her real name and not "Ginger") herself told you to leave, now leave.' Ginger complained of something wrong in her tummy and commanded Satan again to leave in the name of Jesus. She told it to get out of her body and added, 'You're going to leave me.'

It was at this moment, as she started the heavy breathing again, that the Holy Spirit reminded me of a very ancient exorcism prayer we had used in the past. This, I used insofar as I could remember it. It went like this:

'I exorcise you, impious Satan, by the death of Christ on the cross who overcame you. His Blood avails for us. I exorcise you. By penitence already

168

this child of God has restored herself to her true Lord and spurned your yoke. Therefore, I say to you, Satan, be gone. Be exorcised and go, impious Satan, in the Name of Jesus.'

This was followed by a long series of loud screams and the spirit finally yielded and after some 20 minutes, peace descended and Ginger opened her eyes and said, 'It's gone! Thank you, Jesus. Thank you Lord.'

There followed a time of praise and great rejoicing. It has proved to be the finale in a battle that has spanned several years and caused Ginger much sorrow and heartache. She has found that her eyesight is improving – she was extremely short sighted due to not being washed as soon as she was born. The love of God and the reality of Jesus as her personal Lord and Saviour has truly come home to her and she is full of praise and thanksgiving to the Lord Jesus for all that He has done – as are we! Thank you, Jesus!

Chapter 20

The Return of the Lord Jesus Christ for His Bride, the Church

I nearly missed the Truth

Once I was an ordinary 'church-goer', singing Psalms, saying the prayers set out in the Prayer Book, thinking I was well on the road to heaven. But the Lord woke me up. He opened my eyes to see and my ears to hear, and I experienced the 'Book of Acts' as a reality in my life. I have seen many people healed, many delivered from evil spirits and most important event of all: I have witnessed many people being born again – changed from a member of Satan's kingdom of darkness to a member of the glorious kingdom of light of the Lord Jesus. All this proves to me that the Word of God is true, that the Lord Jesus did not submit to the thoughts of His time when He cast out demons and opposed Satan. He knew the truth, and it is the truth that sets free. It is our modern society and education that has gone astray. People do not need meditation, yoga, or mind-emptying to experience peace. It is unnecessary to 'be at one with the universal consciousness' in order to attain true spirituality.

A belief in the Word of God will set them free and they will know the peace of God that passes all understanding.

When I realised that the teaching contained in the Gospels and the descriptions of the Lord's ministry to people were true, I had to face the fact that the Lord's words concerning His return must also be true. He is coming back to this earth just as He said He would. The angel on the day of the Ascension confirmed that Jesus would come back again. Paul attests to it as do the other apostles and in the final book of the Bible, Jesus Himself repeats that He is coming again. There is no doubt about it, He **is** coming again. Just as all the events which had been prophesied concerning His first coming were fulfilled, so will all the prophecies concerning His second coming.

Another real world – and Evolution?

When we have cast out demons we have dealt with, and operated in, the spiritual realm – the supernatural. We could not see the demons but they were there and could use the person's tongue to speak and use the person's body to manifest in. Altogether the Christian life is one of dealing with supernatural things – we speak a prayer and God in heaven hears it – that is supernatural. He sends an angel to do a work for us – that is a supernatural event. He speaks to us by His Spirit – again that is a supernatural event. We are exhorted to walk in the Spirit – another supernatural happening. When we are born again it is a work of God's Holy Spirit and so again we see it is in the supernatural. Many sicknesses and diseases are supernatural in origin and when the evil spirit causing the sickness or disease has been cast out the person is instantly healed.

A thought comes to mind – the God that has power over this world and all spirits does not need millions of years to create this world as the evolutionists would have us believe. It is a lie which poisons people's hearts and drags them away from a belief in the Almighty God and His Son, the Lord Jesus Christ. I would like to ask those scientists who insist on the validity of evolution, why is it that creatures in amber or rock that is alleged to be millions of years old are still the same as those we have today? The same flies, the same spiders, the same fish, the same animals! There is no progress and no evolution in any species. Evolution is unprovable and irrational and you need a fertile imagination to accept it. No, all was created by the Lord God as we are correctly told in Genesis chapters 1 and 2, and they have not changed.

There is more to come

When the Lord Jesus came to the earth He came to be a sacrifice for our sins and to reconcile us to the Father. He shed His blood as a perfect sacrifice to cleanse us from our Adamic sinful nature and all other sins. But this is only a part of our salvation or redemption. As the Apostle Paul says in Romans 8:23, we wait for the redemption of our bodies. The Lord's work of redemption is not fully completed in us as yet. What we have is only an earnest, a down payment in advance as it were. The full completion of His work in us is still to come. This is the glorious truth which we shall yet experience – our bodies will be changed to resemble His body, the one He had after His resurrection. We read in Luke's Gospel something about the Lord Jesus' new body – He could eat, He could be touched, He could be recognised and He could walk through walls and appear and disappear whenever He wanted. He taught the disciples for 40 days about the kingdom of Heaven and opened up the Scriptures about Himself to them and no doubt He talked with them of His return. Also He sent the Holy Spirit to comfort them, to lead them into all truth and to remind them of the things He had told them, and to give them power over all the power of Satan.

Please tell me – When?

There are many Christians who ask, 'When will He come again?' Jesus said that He would come when we are not expecting Him. Again, Jesus spoke of many signs that would come to pass just before His return and when we look at them and at the things going on around us in the world, we have to say it will not be many years before we see the fulfilment of His words. We live in the times of the signs. Israel is back in her homeland, though as yet in unbelief. The kingdom of the antichrist is taking shape very quickly now in Europe and the economies of the European nations are all being geared to a cashless society – that no man might buy or sell, save he has the mark of the beast or the number of his name. That last dreadful empire of iron and clay is slowly coming into being. The 'kings' are giving their authority to it and we can expect to see many more signs being fulfilled. The Holy Spirit is being poured out as never before in human history and the Gospel is being preached in even the remotest parts of the earth via satellites. It will not be long before every nation – it does not say every person – has heard the Gospel and then the end of all the preparations for the kingdom of antichrist will be complete.

We can rejoice, for our redemption draws near. God is using every modern aid in the preaching of the Gospel;

videos, cassettes, tapes, films, cable TV, satellite TV. Millions of Bibles are in circulation and more are being printed, even in little-known languages and dialects. Eastern Europe and what was Russia are responding to the Gospel in thousands; China has a thriving under-ground Church and in South America thousands are coming to know Jesus as Lord and Saviour. Once again the Gospel is being preached with signs following – the sick are being healed and demons cast out. When He was on earth, the Lord Jesus prayed for each one individually. Today evangelists and other preachers are casting out demons from crowds and the sick are being healed as they stand in the meetings. Crowds rush forward towards the end of the meeting to testify of their deliverance or healing. Jesus said,

> *'Greater works will **he** (who believes on Him) do, because I go to My Father.'*

The Bible is full of signs and warnings about the sec-ond coming of our Lord Jesus, both for His Church and to judge the nations and set up the Millennial kingdom of God here on earth. Can we gather an idea from what is written when He will come for His Church? Are there any indications for those living at the time of His return to give some idea whether it is imminent? It seems to me that a number of Scriptures will help us in our search for truth. In our day so much error is being promulgated in these matters – there are many false prophets and christs around, just as Jesus said there would be. Our only sure guide is the Word of God.

Hosea tells us in chapter 6 that Israel will be revived after two days and raised up on the third. But how long is a day in Scripture? In Psalm 90:4 we are told that a thousand years in the sight of God are like yesterday when it is past. Peter puts it the other way round and says that with the Lord, one day is like a thousand years and later that a thousand years are like one day. The Lord Jesus also gave us an indication of when He could be expected to return. Some Pharisees came to Him one day and advised Him to leave the area, for Herod, they said, wanted to kill Him. Jesus' reply is very illuminating. (It is recorded in Luke's Gospel chapter 13.)

> *'Go, tell that fox, "Behold, I cast out demons and perform cures today and tomorrow, and the third day I shall be perfected." Nevertheless I must journey today, tomorrow, and the day following; for it cannot be that a prophet should perish outside of Jerusalem.'*

Here, Jesus is speaking of two different events. Firstly He refers to the Church Age, an age in which the Church would carry on His ministry of casting out demons and healing the sick; then He refers to His being 'perfected'. I believe that Jesus is here referring to the wedding feast with His Bride, the Church. No Bridegroom is perfected without His Bride and the Church is the Bride of Christ. After the Rapture and Judgement Seat of Christ there will come the Wedding Breakfast and the Lord Jesus will be perfected in the sense intended in our passage from Luke. He then went on to speak of the time left to Him here on this earth before He would go to Jerusalem to be crucified.

The Lord's Calendar

In Genesis the story of creation and how God created all in six days and rested the seventh is a picture for the future of the earth as God viewed it then. Six days, then

a rest day – the glorious kingdom of God here on earth –
the day of rest spoken of in Hebrews. If we accept the
creation record, as we surely must, then we are very
nearly at the end of the sixth day, which is to be followed by a seventh day. Adam was created almost 6,000
years ago, or six days by God's reckoning. When Adam
and Eve ate the forbidden fruit they died spiritually
there and then but they lived on for almost a thousand
years. Yet God had said that they would die on the day
they ate of that forbidden fruit. This appears to be an
anomaly, until we look at it from God's point of view,
when a thousand years is as one day. Adam and Eve did
indeed die the day they ate of the fruit of the tree, for a
thousand years are as a day.

We find another Old Testament statement of time in
the Lord's calendar in Daniel chapter 10. Here Daniel
speaks of a 'certain Man', one 'having the likeness of a
man', who tells Daniel that there is a Scripture of Truth.
From this it would seem that all things are firstly noted
in Heaven and then worked out here on earth. If we look
at Isaiah 53, for example, we read in verse 7,

'He was led as a lamb to the slaughter.'

John the Baptist takes up this expression when he sees
the Lord Jesus approaching him and says,

*'Behold! The Lamb of God who takes away the sin of
the world!'*   (John 1:29)

From these two Scriptures we see that we are first of all
given the detail in Isaiah, then the Lord Jesus comes and
lives out what has been foretold. That the Lord God is
in control of earth's history is unquestionable. Jeremiah
prophesied that the Jews would go into captivity in

Babylon and would remain there for 70 years, after which they would be allowed to return to their homeland. Daniel had made a study of Jeremiah's prophecies and realised that the 70 years he spoke of were fulfilled – this was in the first year of Darius, a Mede who had become king of the Chaldeans in Babylon. So Daniel sets himself to seek God for the release of His people and the angel Gabriel is sent to give Daniel a brief world history. Gabriel appears to be involved when events are related to the Lord Jesus. He was sent to Zacharias to announce the birth of John the Baptist, the forerunner of the Lord Jesus and to Mary to tell her that she was the one chosen by God to be the mother of Jesus.

Daniel – a special Man of God

Gabriel reveals to Daniel that:

> '70 weeks are determined for your people and for your holy city, to finish the transgression, to make an end of sins, to make reconciliation for iniquity, to bring in everlasting righteousness, to seal up vision and prophecy, and to anoint the Most Holy.'
>
> (Daniel 9:24)

The words 'weeks' can be literally translated 'seven'. Thus we have 70 sevens, or 490 years. In verse 25 Gabriel tells Daniel that there are to be 69 weeks from the going forth of the command to restore and rebuild Jerusalem until Messiah the Prince. But that still leaves the question of the 70th week, or seven years. In verse 27 of the same chapter we read more about this final week. There will be one who will make a covenant with the Jews and then break it in the middle of the seven years.

This man is called a prince in verse 26 and it is revealed that **his people** will destroy Jerusalem and the Temple. This was fulfilled under Titus in AD 70. However, verse 26 spoke of the prince who is to come. This man will be from the same empire as the 'people' of verse 26. From this we see that the empire which would destroy Jerusalem and the Temple will reappear in the last days. We also see that while this ruler may initially deal peacefully with Israel, he will subsequently break the covenant in the middle of the 'week'. The prophet Isaiah refers to this covenant in these words:

> *'Your covenant with death will be annulled, and your agreement with Sheol will not stand; when the overflowing scourge passes through, then you will be trampled down by it.'* (Isaiah 28:18)

From this passage we also learn that there is going to be a time of great trouble for Israel. God is going to use this ruler to scourge His people and there will be no escape, for the scourge is an overflowing one.

The period of this overflowing scourge is also known as the Great Tribulation, the time of Jacob's trouble, the Day of Wrath, and the Great and Terrible Day of the Lord, as well as the Day of Vengeance of our God. The Daniel passage tells us the key event which will herald the last seven years – the second half of which will be the Great Tribulation – before Jesus comes to rule over the earth. That event is the preparation for the signing of the covenant 'with many for one week'. The signing of the covenant itself is the start of the countdown of those seven years. It is our firm belief that this time is not far off and that we shall see the events which lead up to this time taking place in our lifetime. Jesus said in John 9:4 that:

'I must work the works of Him who sent Me while it is day; the night is coming when no one can work.'

There have been almost 2,000 years in which to preach the Gospel with signs following – years which were not revealed to Daniel. It is still day and we can still work but the night is fast approaching. This period, often called the Church Age, was not revealed to Daniel because the Church was a mystery – hidden until New Testament times.

Is Jesus coming for you?

Daniel was told that after the 62 weeks (434 years) had expired Messiah would be cut off. And so it was, for the Lord Jesus rode into Jerusalem exactly at that time on a donkey. They acclaimed Him on that day but disclaimed Him not many days later. But, although crucified, dead and buried, on the third day He rose triumphant from the tomb and ascended into heaven. As Hebrews tells us,

'Christ was offered once to bear the sins of many.'

He bore our sins and was cut off, not for Himself, but for us. The disciples were told on the day of the ascension that Jesus would come in exactly the same manner as they saw Him go. This raises the question, who will He be coming for and why? He will be coming for those who are eagerly waiting for Him and for no-one else. Those who deny the truth of the Rapture, for example, will only know about it when we have gone. Those who are not waiting for Him will miss it, as will those who are only matter-of-factly waiting for Him. And **why** is He coming? He is coming to deliver those who are

179

eagerly waiting for Him from the Tribulation, the rule of antichrist, the time of God's wrath and judgement upon the world because of their unbelief and rejection of the Lord Jesus. All is being prepared for that great event. The whole world is being prepared in one way or another. The fourth kingdom which Daniel saw in an earlier vision, distinct from all the others before it, is about to reappear. The first distinct kingdom was the Roman Empire, distinct from all the others because it was imperialistic. The nations which comprised the three earlier kingdoms were not imperialistic. They did not send one of their own race to be king over the peoples they conquered, but appointed a local man to be king. The Romans on the other hand always sent someone from Rome to be governor of the nations they conquered.

Wrath or Glory?

Some people teach that a time of great tribulation is coming upon the earth and that the Church of Jesus Christ will have to go through it. Many will lose their lives because of their commitment to the Lord Jesus. Yes, dark days are coming upon the earth, when the man of sin will rule the whole world – that period known as the time of Jacob's trouble, the Great Tribulation, the Day of Wrath – but I do not believe the Church of Jesus Christ will be here on the earth to witness it or go through it. Romans 5:9 tells us that we shall be saved from wrath through Him (Jesus) and in chapter 9:22–24 we read,

'What if God, wanting to show His wrath and to make His power known, endured with much longsuffering

the vessels of wrath prepared for destruction, and
that He might make known the riches of His glory
on the vessels of mercy, which He had prepared
beforehand for glory, even us whom He called, not of
the Jews only, but also of the Gentiles?'

Does this not clearly show that some are doomed to
destruction through His wrath while there are vessels of
mercy prepared for glory? Then again in 1 Thessalonians
1:10 we are told that Jesus delivers us from the wrath to
come and in chapter 5:9 we find that God did not
appoint us to wrath, but to obtain salvation (deliverance) through our Lord Jesus Christ.

On the other hand Ephesians 2:1–3 says:

'And you He made alive, who were dead in tres-
passes and sins, in which you once walked according
to the course of this world, according to the prince of
the power of the air, the spirit who now works in the
sons of disobedience, among whom also we all once
conducted ourselves in the lusts of our flesh,
fulfilling the desires of the flesh and of the mind,
and were by nature children of wrath, just as the
others.'

We **were** children of wrath, but are no longer, Paul says.
Those who have not been made alive, according to this
passage, are the sons of disobedience, and in chapter 5:6
Paul tells them that the wrath of God comes upon the
sons of disobedience. This theme is repeated in Paul's
letter to the Colossians, for in chapter 3:6 he writes,

'Because of these things (fornication, uncleanness,
passion, evil desire, and covetousness, which is

idolatry) the wrath of God is coming upon the sons of disobedience.'

It is interesting that in the Book of Revelation, chapters 4 to 20 where the wrath of God is poured out on the earth in judgement – the Great Tribulation – the Church is not mentioned anywhere other than in heaven.

The Church is going to be taken away from this earth before the Great and Terrible Day of the Lord. Jesus is coming again for His own, but not openly. It will be as a thief in the night. Paul, writing to the Church in Thessalonica, penned this:

> *'For this we say to you by the word of the Lord* (he had received a Divine revelation concerning this event, as is evident by his use of the term "by the word of the Lord"), *that we who are alive and remain until the coming of the Lord will by no means precede those who are asleep* (dead). *For the Lord Himself will descend from heaven with a shout, with the voice of an archangel, and with the trumpet of God. And the dead in Christ will rise first. Then we who are alive and remain shall be caught up together with them in the clouds to meet the Lord in the air. And thus we shall always be with the Lord.'*

This passage is addressed to Christians, not to the world in general. The Lord Jesus spoke in similar vein after the death of Lazarus when He met Martha outside the town. Jesus said:

> *'I am the resurrection and the life. He who believes in Me, though he may die, he shall live. And whoever lives and believes in Me shall never die.'*

182

In this passage Jesus clearly shows that there will be some who die and yet they shall live, while others who believe in Him and live shall never die – that is they are alive at His return for His Bride, the Church (John 11:25, 26).

Paul received a special revelation

(1 Thessalonians 4:15–18)

God has set out a programme for the Tribulation and Paul had one for the Rapture by revelation from the Lord Jesus. Some of the Thessalonian believers were concerned about those of their number who had died – would they miss out on the Rapture? They knew there was a Rapture, but how did it affect those who had died? Paul sets out to answer this question and gives God's programme as it relates to both dead and living believers. It comprises seven distinct steps. Firstly, he points out, it is Jesus Himself who comes from the Heaven of heavens to our atmospheric heaven. Orbiting space probes, spacecraft and satellites will not interfere with this for it will be in the spiritual realm, not the physical. Secondly, Paul tells them that Jesus Himself will give a shout. The word used here has the connotation of a military command. When Jesus stood at the tomb of Lazarus He *'cried with a loud voice, "Lazarus, come forth!"'* I believe that if Jesus had just called out *'Come forth!'*, **all** the dead would have been raised. When He comes for His own He will call in such a way that only the dead and living saints will hear it. We are then told that there is the voice of an archangel. We often find in the Scriptures that angels are used to put God's plans into effect. Gabriel had been sent by God to Daniel straightaway but had been resisted on the way until

God sent another angel to help him. Perhaps the archangel will repeat Christ's shout. At the same time comes the trumpet call of God – a reminder of the Feast of Trumpets, the next event on God's calendar! Trumpets were used as a summons to battle or worship and Israel's Feast of Trumpets was followed some time later by the Day of Atonement, then the Feast of Tabernacles. After this came the Feast of Dedication and finally Purim which celebrated the rescue from Haman's plot to destroy the nation. Next time it will celebrate their deliverance from antichrist. There is a much deeper meaning to the various Feasts of Israel than we realise and studying them can be most rewarding.

Paul then tells the Thessalonians that the dead in Christ will rise first. This resurrection is limited to true born-again believers, not nominal Christians. Nor does it include unbelievers or the Old Testament saints who are already in Heaven. Unbelievers will await the Great White Throne judgement. They are resurrected just before that awful event, then any whose names are not written in the Book of Life are thrown into the Lake of Fire. We beg those of you who are reading this book to make sure your name is written in the Lamb's Book of Life by accepting Jesus Christ as your Lord and Saviour. Confess that you are a sinner and need His salvation, so freely offered to you, for which He died. Renounce all the hidden works of darkness, deceit and sin and repent before Him, claiming His shed blood for the cleansing of your guilt. Invite Him to be Lord of your life, to come and take control of your heart and mind. Call upon His Holy Spirit to come and take up His rightful place in you and make you a true Child of God. That is the only way to be written in the Lamb's Book of Life. You will then be numbered among those blessed ones who will hear His shout and that of the archangel and the trumpet of God, whenever that comes.

The gathering of the dead to meet the Lord in the air is not a solitary event, for we who are left alive and remain until the Lord comes will be caught up with them in the air. That is the sixth event in the Rapture. Our mortal body must put on immortality, Paul told the Corinthian church, and we will, in the twinkling of an eye. As we leave this earth, a miracle will take place in a moment, quicker than eye can see. Our earthly body will be transformed into the likeness of His glorious Body. Perhaps it will be like the one the Lord Jesus had on the Mount of Transfiguration? We are not told, but it will be beyond anything we can conceive of now. The final event of the Rapture is that we meet the Lord in the air and are united with Him for evermore. Well might John the apostle say that if we have this hope in us we purify ourselves. Without holiness, no one will see the Lord. We do well to bear this in mind as we see the Day approaching.

Reader, are you ready for this great event commonly called the Rapture? If not, we beg you to get ready. Confess, renounce and repent of all your sins and claim the Blood of the Lord Jesus to cleanse you. Accept Him as your Lord and Saviour now. Why not say the following prayer and know for certain you are going to be part of the Bride of Christ for whom He is soon returning?

'Holy Father in Heaven, I come to you in Jesus' Name. I confess that I am a sinner and that I need your salvation. I claim the Blood of Jesus to cleanse me and set me free. Satan, I renounce you and all your works and I will follow you, Lord Jesus, from this day forward. Holy Spirit, come into my heart, come into my life; let me know of a surety I have been born again and made a child of God. Lord Jesus, I thank you for dying for me and I look forward to meeting you soon.'

Now join a Bible-believing Church.

Appendix

Have you taken part in occult practices or been present when such practices were performed? Have you been present when any paranormal activity of any kind, including astral travel, took place? Have you ever used any occult object for any reason? To help you, we give below a list of some of the more common forms of occult practices and objects. If you are aware that you have been involved with any of these, you will need to confess, renounce and repent of such practices and seek ministry for deliverance.

Acupuncture
Amulets
Ankh
Anthroposophy
Apparitions
Astral travel
Astrology
Atheism
Augury
Automatic writing
Birth stones

Black arts
Black magic
Black mass
Blood pacts
Card laying
Chain letters
Charms
Clairaudience
Clairvoyance
Conjuration
Copper bracelet

Coven
Crystal gazing
Death magic
Demon worship
Divination
Drugs
Druidism
Dungeons and Dragons
Eastern meditation
Enchanting
ESP
Fetishes
Findhorn
Firewalking
Floating trumpets
Fortune telling
Freemasonry
Gypsy curses
Halloween
Handwriting analysis
Hard rock music
Heavy metal music
Heresies
Hexagrams
Homoeopathy
Horoscopes
Horse shoe
Hypnotism
Idols
Incantations
I Ching
Iridology
Judo
Kabbala
Levitation

Lucky charms
Magic healing
Martial arts
Mascots
Materialisations
Meditation
Mediums
Mental telepathy
Mesmerism
Metaphysics
Mind control
Mind reading
Moon-mancy
Necromancy
New Age
Occult games
Occult literature
Omens
Ouija boards
Pagan fetishes
Pagan religious objects
Pagan rites
Palmistry
Parakinesis
Parapsychology
Pendulum swinging
Phrenology
Planchette
Pornography
Precognition
Psychic healing
Psychic powers
Psychoanalysis
Psychography
Psychometry

Radiesthesia
Reflexology
Religious relics
Role playing games
Science of mind
Seances
Second sight
Self-hypnosis
Significant days
Signs of the Zodiac
Sorcery
Spells
Spirit knockings
Spiritism
Spiritual healing
Spoon bending

Star signs
Table lifting
Table rapping
Talisman
Tarot cards
Tea leaf reading
Telekinesis
Telepathy
Thought transference
Trances
Transvestism
Voodoo
White magic
Witchcraft
Yoga
Zodiac charms

Many Christians are superstitious, yet this is in direct contrast to the Scriptures. The question is: 'In what or in whom is your trust?' There is no such thing as 'luck'. If you are, or have been, superstitious, you will need to confess, renounce and repent of these practices and claim the Blood of Jesus for your cleansing. We list below some of the more commonly held superstitions.

Astrology: a belief that the stars and/or planets can influence your life. Wearing Bible verses to ward off evil. A black cat crossing one's path means good luck. A bride must wear something old, something new, something borrowed, something blue on her wedding day. Burning ears mean someone is talking about you.

Crossed knives are unlucky, as is a clock stopping, foretelling a death in the family. Wearing a copper bracelet against rheumatism and answering chain letters. Using crossed fingers for good luck.

Finding a four-leaf clover is good luck, but flowers from a cemetery are bad luck. Not doing certain things on Fridays – especially if it is the 13th. First footing in Scotland is a superstition.

Many will not wear green, as it is considered unlucky, whereas a horseshoe is considered to bring good luck. An itchy hand means you have something good coming.

If you give a knife or scissors to someone you must also give a coin, else a friendship will be cut. Kissing the Blarney stone and kissing under the mistletoe are also superstitions. Walking under a ladder is considered unlucky as is the breaking of a mirror (seven years bad luck). However, 'Monday's child is fair of face, Tuesday's child ... '

It is unlucky to look at the new moon through glass and you should also turn your silver at first sighting. Then there are so-called lucky or unlucky numbers, such as 13; everything goes in threes. If you want good luck all day then see a pin and pick it up. A picture falling off the wall indicates a death in the house but finding a piece of white heather is good luck.

Sneezes have a superstitious significance – once a wish, twice a kiss, three times a letter. When someone sneezes you will often hear folk say 'Bless you.' This dates back to the plague and was supposed to ward off that terrible sickness. We have all heard of the wishing well and there is also the wish-bone from the chicken or turkey. Spilt salt must be thrown over the shoulder (does it matter which one?)

Then we have the 'touch wood' brigade who aim to ward off evil, as well as those who refuse to open an umbrella in a house for fear of bringing bad luck on it. Car owners will often fix a St Christopher medallion to their vehicle in an attempt to ward off accidents. Squeaky shoes, of course, have not been paid for.

All these and every other superstition – there are hundreds of them – are against the Word of God and bring us into bondage to spiritual forces, for we are handing our will over to them. Often we will cause the superstition to come true by our actions, quite un-wittingly.

If you have indulged in any superstitious practice you should now confess, renounce and repent of it, claiming the Blood of Jesus to cleanse you and set you free. You should also command every spirit of superstition to leave you in Jesus' name.